VOICES from the DEAD

Voices From The Dead

The Dark Rituals and Hidden Worship of the Masonic Lodge

TEXE MARRS

RiverCrest Publishing
4819 R.O. Drive, Suite 102, Spicewood, TX 78669

Voices From The Dead

Second Printing 2019

Copyright © 2018. Published by RiverCrest Publishing, 4819 R.O. Drive, Suite 102, Spicewood, Texas 78669.

Cover design: Texe Marrs and Sandra Myers

Printed in the United States of America

Library of Congress Catalog Card Number 201894567

Categories: 1. Religion   2. Freemasonry
              3. Christianity   4. Judaism

ISBN 978-1-930004-17-7

(Note: In this book, the Kabbalah is sometimes spelled Kabala, Cabala, or by another variation. The author generally uses the spelling in the source being quoted.)

"Examine us in depth—we have nothing to hide."

— James T. Tresner, 33°, in the
foreword to *Is it True What
They Say About Freemasonry?*
(Masonic Service Association, 1994)

OTHER BOOKS BY TEXE MARRS

Blood Covenant With Destiny: The Babylonian Talmud, the Jewish Kabbalah, and the Power of Prophecy

Hell's Mirror: Global Empire of the Illuminati Builders

Feast of the Beast

The Destroyer: The Antichrist Is At Hand

Holy Serpent of the Jews: The Rabbis' Secret Plan for Satan to Crush Their Enemies and Vault the Jews to Global Dominion

Robot Alchemy: Androids, Cyborgs, and the Magic of Artificial Life

Pastors and Churches Gone Wild: America's Christian Establishment Has Gone Berserk!

DNA Science and the Jewish Bloodline

Conspiracy of the Six-Pointed Star: Eye-Opening Revelations and Forbidden Knowledge About Israel, the Jews, Zionism, and the Rothschilds

Conspiracy World: A Truthteller's Compendium of Eye-Opening Revelations and Forbidden Knowledge

Mysterious Monuments: Encyclopedia of Secret Illuminati Designs, Masonic Architecture, and Occult Places

Codex Magica: Secret Signs, Mysterious Symbols and Hidden Codes of the Illuminati

Days of Hunger, Days of Chaos: The Coming Great Food Shortages in America

Project L.U.C.I.D.: The Beast 666 Universal Human Control System

Circle of Intrigue: The Hidden Inner Circle of the Global Illuminati Conspiracy

Dark Majesty: The Secret Brotherhood and the Magic of a Thousand Points of Light

New Age Cults and Religions

Millennium: Peace, Promises, and the Day They Take Our Money Away

Ravaged By the New Age: Satan's Plan to Destroy Our Kids

Mystery Mark of the New Age: Satan's Design for World Dominion

Dark Secrets of the New Age: Satan's Plan for a One World Religion

For additional books by RiverCrest Publishing see page 156

For additional information we highly recommend the following website:
www.powerofprophecy.com

TABLE OF
Contents

He Speaks From His Coffin to the Masonic Candidates. Who is This Man?

- He is said to be the Father of international Freemasonry.

- Albert Pike, 33°, boasted: He holds "The Keys of the Present, the Past, and the Future."

- He authored a mystical book widely acclaimed in modern Judaism. The Jews say that a team of "angels" dictated this book to him.

- His teachings are found in the Jewish Talmud and are considered "Law" to modern-day Jews. Among his most famous teachings: "The best of the Christians—Kill!"

- A pedophile, he taught it is acceptable for a high priest to have sex with three year-old girls.

- He is honored today in the Masonic Lodge's 30th degree ritual in which he lies in a coffin and directs the initiation of candidates, requiring oaths of them to abandon their faith and adopt the Mystery religion of kabbalistic Freemasonry.

Who is this man? Why do Masons say his famous Zohar and Kabbalah are far superior to the Holy Bible?

The incredible truth about this mysterious satanic disciple is revealed in the pages of **Voices From the Dead.**

ACKNOWLEDGEMENTS AND INTRODUCTION

"And so, whether we worship at the shrines and embrace the doctrines of Zoroaster or Mohammed or Confucius or Moses or Buddha or those of the Christian world, we know that there moves among us every day a timeless Force, greater and stronger than ourselves..."

—Henry C. Clausen, 33°
Sovereign Grand Commander,
(Supreme Mother Council, 1980)
Emergence of the Mystical

The above statement is typical of Masonry's leaders. It indicates Freemasonry's worship of a mysterious *Force* that exists in the world. This Force, says Masonry's leaders, is neither Christian nor of another world faith. Its' names are derived strictly from the Jewish Kabbalah and the ancient primitive religion prescribed in the rituals and ceremonies of Freemasonry. The worship of this Force predates Christianity and, claim the Masons, is able to make men divine gods. What is this *Force*? Is it of God or of Satan? Can we access the dead to answer these questions? That

11

is the subject matter of this book.

One Masonic authority, quoted in this book, refers to this Force as the *"Seething energies of Lucifer."* This, regrettably, represents the doctrine of Freemasonry. We will closely examine this ungodly doctrine in these pages, but I wish to declare now, up front, that Masonry is far off the mark in it's strange philosophy.

I believe that, for Christians, it is only necessary to keep in mind these two important Scriptures when gauging the truth and untruth found in Freemasonry.

1. Jesus our Lord stated: *"I am the way, the truth, and the life: no man cometh unto the Father, but by me."* *(John 14:6)*

2. The Apostle Paul wrote: *"That at the name of Jesus every knee should bow, of things in heaven, and things in earth, and things under the earth; And that every tongue should confess that Jesus Christ is Lord, to the glory of God the Father."* *(Philippians 2:10,11)*

Freemasonry adamantly opposes both these scriptural truths. Both are at the very foundation of true Christianity. Thus we know that the Masonic Lodge is decidedly *not* of the Christian faith.

Acknowledgements and Gratitude

I wish to acknowledge and give gratitude for the many Christian researchers investigating the field of Freemasonry. Without your outstanding efforts, my own research would be severely impeded. Thank you so very much!

I would especially like to thank my dear friend, James L. Holly, M.D. Dr. Holly is not only a premier medical doctor from Beaumont, Texas, he has pioneered the way for many to examine the lies and deceptions of Freemasonry. In the 1990s, Dr. Holly was a leader in the Southern Baptist Convention movement to expose Freemasonry and prove conclusively that it is not compatible with Christianity. His efforts, I believe, were stunningly successful and many Masons consequently renounced their membership in the Masonic Lodge. These men were freed from the demonic grip of Masonry and their souls cleansed. I am convinced that when he goes to heaven, Dr. Holly will meet many of these men and truly understand how many lives he has saved.

Dr. Holly is also the Christian inspiration for this book. It was from reading his excellent volumes, *The Southern Baptist Convention and Freemasonry*, that I came upon the name "Simeon Bar Yochai." As far as I can tell, Dr. Holly is one of the first Christian researchers to connect Rabbi Bar Yochai with Masonic ritual. Having written several key books recently on the kabbalistic religion, I immediately recognized the important role played by one of Judaism's most famous authorities, Simeon Bar Yochai (*Rabbi* Simeon Bar Yochai) in Freemasonry. He is author of the Jewish Kabbalah and its component book, *The Zohar*. This is a primary source— you can call these books the "Bible" of Freemasonry.

Dr. Holly's accurate exposure of one of Judaism's most famous ancient rabbis, Rabbi Simeon Bar Yochai, is extremely important. It highlights the direct links between the kabbalistic religion of Judaism and Freemasonry. Most

Christian investigations of the Masonic Lodge omit mentions of this key link. The researchers do not wish to impugn Judaism. Some are afraid of being unfairly branded an anti-Semite. They fail to report the clear statements of Freemasonry's founders who heap effusive praise on Judaism's occult Kabbalah and give credit to the Kabbalah for Freemasonry's doctrines, practices, and rituals.

Voices From the Dead examines Freemasonry as it really is. This book does not flinch from telling the truth. Only by discovering the truth about Freemasonry, its Mystery religion aspects, and its close links with rabbinical Judaism can men be set free from the subtlety and deception inherent in this, the world's largest secret society.

My hope in writing this book is that many Masons will understand the awful truth about the Masonic religion and renounce it. I pray, too, that those considering becoming a Mason will reconsider in light of the truths found in these pages.

A special note for fellow Christians. We must understand that some entrapped in the Masonic Lodge are victims. Few are outright Lucifer Worshippers. Most are hoodwinked by Freemasonry and brainwashed, degree by degree. Remember, we war against the powers of darkness, the demonic forces, that bind these men to the Lie. We must be firm in our opposition to these dark forces while being sensitive to those who are deceived. It is entirely possible that some may be reached with God's Truth.

In Christian Love,
Texe Marrs
Austin, Texas

Freemasonry: The Riddle Solved

"It is a riddle wrapped in a mystery inside an enigma."
—*Sir Winston Churchill*

E ngland's late Prime Minister, Sir Winston Churchill, is noted for many great speeches he gave. But perhaps the most notable is the radio broadcast he delivered on October 1, 1939. Referring to the future action of communist Russia, Churchill said he could not forecast such action, "It is," he remarked, *"a riddle wrapped in a mystery inside an enigma."*

Nevertheless, the wise Prime Minister offered a "key" to understanding, and in light of world history in subsequent years, that key was proven correct.

The key to understanding Russia's actions precedent to and including the World War II years and beyond was, in fact, earlier revealed by Churchill in *The London*

Chronicle of February 13, 1920. There, the then British Secretary of War, Mr. Churchill, had charged Jews with originating the gospel of antichrist and of engineering a worldwide conspiracy for the overthrow of civilization.

That Churchill was correct in providing this important "key" was admitted by Rabbi Stephen Wise, the most famous Jewish rabbi in America during this era. Asked about the meaning of "communism," Wise retorted, *"Some Call it Communism. I call it Judaism."* Thus was the riddle solved.

Freemasonry's Secrets

Now we come to the riddle of Freemasonry, popularly called the "Masonic Lodge." According to the Masons, of which there are some 20 to 30 million gentlemen affiliated across the globe, Freemasonry, too, is *"a riddle wrapped in a mystery inside an enigma."* C. Lenning, a German who served as Grand Master of the Masonic Lodge, in his *Encyclopedia of Freemasonry* for example, boasted, *"Freemasonry has no secrets, but it is a secret."*

"Our Secrets, however, have so far been safeguarded," said the puffed up Mr. Lenning, "no one has yet dared to overstep this line."

What utter nonsense, what pure drivel is Mr. Lenning's confident assertion. Yet, leader after Masonic leader asserts the same. They brag, "We cannot tell you our secrets." They have even taken bloody oaths, contrary to the Word of God, pledging their lives—and necks—that they will forever preserve Freemasonry's dire secrets. Masons pride themselves on their dogged determination to "conceal and never reveal" these secrets. They lie, obfuscate, dodge, and, to use their own term, "hoodwink" the public and even their own members.

Real "Christian" gentlemen, wouldn't you say? Of course, Jesus Christ advised us never to take any oath of any kind *(Matthew 5:34)*. As for his own secrets Christ had none.

> *"Jesus answered him, I spake openly to the world and in secret have I said nothing."*
>
> —*John 18:20*

I Divulge the Secret of Freemasonry

Therefore, in the spirit of Christ Jesus, I reveal to you exactly what Freemasonry is, i.e. its "secret."

> Freemasonry is an *"Ancient Mystery Religion,"* whose members are initiated in the worship of—get ready for it—*Satan!*

Thus is the riddle, the secret and secrets, of Freemasonry and its perverse "Masonic Lodge" solved. But I am not the first to divulge their secret.

This riddle has actually long been solved. Lady Queensborough revealed it in her classic textbook, *Occult Theocracy* (1933), when she wrote:

> "Every Lodge is a Synagogue of Satan and its rituals Sorcery."

It should be noted that Lady Queensborough provided us with a further sub-key to understanding Freemasonry.

She says it is a *"Synagogue of Satan"* thus informing us of its malevolant Judaic aspect. More on this later.

Now, in this present volume, I echo Lady Queensborough, and I confirm also the findings of such great modern-day Christian researchers as James L. Holly, M.D., A. Ralph Epperson, John Ankerberg, Jack Fisher, Ed Decker, Harold Berry and Reginald C. Haupt, Jr. All of these individuals, and many others besides, have discovered the *"Satan Connection"* with Freemasonry and reported it in their many outstanding writings and speeches.

Let me repeat then: Freemasonry is an *Ancient Mystery religion.* It is, moreover, a *worship* of many deities, most of whom are mere fronts, or dark angels, assigned to the chief god, the hidden entity we know as *Satan*, or *Lucifer*. And a Masonic Lodge is a *church, synagogue*, or *temple* of that god. The worship or rituals carried on at the Lodge is, in fact, sorcery, which we can also term as communion with devils.

Attempts to Deny: Laughable and Should be Scorned

This description of Freemasonry cannot be denied, and I find the attempted denial by Masons and their deceitful propaganda very juvenile, even laughable.

Some apologists for Masons insist one must become a Mason in order to understand the Masonic Lodge. But one does not need to become a Mason to understand the depraved nature of this seedy and soiled organization, just as one need not become a rapist to understand the criminal act of rape or engage in murder to comprehend this heinous crime. So when you and I are accosted by contemptible persons making such a foolish assertion, we can only laugh at their pitiful attempts to divert from the truth.

Judges, juries and prosecuting attorneys are established to determine the guilt of a rapist or murderer. We thus allow reasonable people to hear the available evidence and decide. Exactly in this manner can you and I and others determine whether Freemasonry is an ancient Mystery religion in which members practice sorcery by worship of a god we know as Satan. Of course, the Mason will claim their deity is not Satan, but is instead a shadowy, ineffable god known by them as the *Grand Architect of the Universe.* They will then dance and cavort about pretending that the Grand Architect isn't his real name— that must be kept secret, known only by Masons and adepts—they will then insist that a number of dumb and lame substitutes will suffice for their deity's "real name."

Poor Satan, he is so pitiful the Mason has to go to incredible lengths to avoid naming him. But to no avail, because anyone truly schooled in Mystery religions, or in other Luciferian cults, can quickly identify the Masonic deity. Why, he is Satan, of course.

How to Determine His Name and Identity

My recognition of the occult nature of Freemasonry came about through my study of Mystery religions similar to Freemasonry. Neither I nor my family has any connection with the Masonic fraternity. Freemasonry was common in East Texas where I was raised and every town and city seemingly had its own Masonic Lodge. I did notice that some of the Lodges had strange symbols on their buildings and even displayed various Egyptian statues. I was told that Freemasons were "good people," and the men I met who were Masons appeared to fit that description.

I joined the U. S. Air Force at the early age of 18 and stayed on for a career, serving as an officer in Asia, Europe and throughout North America. While in the Air Force, I had no association whatever with Freemasons. In 1986, having retired after 20 years in Air Force blue and achieving two college degrees, I had the opportunity and privilege to author several important books.

One of these books, *Dark Secrets of the New Age*, examined the burgeoning New Age movement in some detail. In the book I surveyed and analyzed the New Age movement, contrasting its tenets with those of traditional Christianity. *Dark Secrets of the New Age* quotes over 1,000 New Age authorities and experts in a variety of cults and religions. As I reported in its pages, the New Age is an umbrella movement comprised of hundreds of *Mystery Religions* and affiliated cult organizations and groups.

Dark Secrets of the New Age quickly became an overwhelming success and a #1 Christian bestseller. Its success and the need for this information encouraged me to author a number of other follow-up reference books on the topic of New Age Mystery Religions, cults, organizations, and personalities.

In all these groups I discovered several common characteristics. First, their doctrines, teachings, and rituals are based primarily on ancient *Mystery Religions*.

There was little that was "new" in these many New

Age groups. Their origins could be traced back to ancient Egypt, Babylon, Greece, Rome, and even to North Africa, Asia Minor, and to the Orient.

What's more, almost every single group is based on the structure and belief system of the ancient *Jewish Kabbalah*. The Jewish Kabbalah, meanwhile, is itself a Mystery religion, emanating out of Babylon where the Jews were held captive for many years during the time of the prophets Jeremiah and Daniel and also borrowing from the Canaanite pagan religions. The Kabbalah is also imitative of the ancient Egyptian religion of the pharaoic nation where the Jews were exiled. It is far from Old Testament religion, but it is an integral and inseparable part of the religion of Judaism, which is based on the man-made traditions of the Talmud and the Kabbalah.

What is really fascinating—and instructive—is that Freemasonry is so often given as the source for many New Age religious groups, practices, and rituals. When visiting a New Age occult bookstore one can quickly get the feeling that you are in the Master Library of Freemasonry at the House of the Temple in Washington, D.C. Indeed, at the time I authored *Dark Secrets of the New Age*, the title of the periodic Masonic publication that goes out to its members was entitled *New Age*, and a book just published at the time by the Scottish Rite, was *Emergence of the Mystical*, written by the then Sovereign Grand Commander, Henry C. Clausen, 33°.

The entire New Age movement, therefore, is not new at all, but, rather, is the culmination of hundreds of years of teaching and practice of Freemasonry. To discover, too, that Freemasonry and these many evidences of the

Henry C. Clausen, 33°, a recent Sovereign Grand Commander of Scottish Rite Freemasonry, wrote a New Age mystical book published by the Masonic Order entitled, *Emergence of the Mystical*.

New Age movement are based primarily on ancient Mystery Religions and on the associated Jewish Kabbalah was significant as well.

If a person first studies the Jewish Kabbalah, then tacks on top the study of ancient Mystery religions throughout history, he or she can be assured that he will have learned the so-called *Lost Keys*, or *Secrets of Freemasonry*. He will have solved the riddle.

And exactly what *knowledge* will such a student of the Ancient Mystery Religions, including the Jewish Kabbalah, have attained? To wit, that:

> "Freemasonry is an *Ancient Mystery Religion*, based on the Jewish Kabbalah, with *sorcery* as its *rituals*. Its adepts are initiated in the *worship* of *Satan*."

Masonic Knowledge Revealed by Top Masonic Authorities

Please notice, dear friends that in this opening chapter of *Voices From the Dead*, I have not attempted to keep from you, the reader, the answers to the supposed Freemasonry riddle. You deserve to know the horrific and deceptive secrets of the Masonic Lodge, and I have told you what they are. I explained that my conclusions are based on over thirty years of my own investigation and research and on the superlative efforts of many other Christian researchers.

But, like those in other cults and fake religions, masonry continues to fight and argue against these proven allegations of satanic skullduggery on its part. Consequently, I have decided to go out and survey the so-called "Lost Keys" of Freemasonry, as confided in their own, authoritative reference books.

Masonry has officially been around since 1717, when the satanic group was first formally organized in Great Britain. Of course, its roots, say the Masons themselves, can be traced all the way back to the primitive era of

Nimrod, Semiramis, and the woebegone Tower of Babel in Babylon. I have gone back and consulted all the great authorities and experts of Masonry. Here, in this book you will read what the top Masons themselves have to say.

△ Is Freemasonry an ancient Mystery religion?

△ Are its rituals based on sorcery and magic?

△ Do its doctrines come out of the ancient and modern Jewish Kabbalah?

△ And most important, do high-level Freemasons worship none other than Satan as Lord?

Freemasonry Authorities Answer

The many celebrated, lavishly decorated, and proud members and poobahs of the world's largest Secret Society will answer these questions. Their own speeches and declarations will inform you. They are quoted in the book you now read. After reading this book, *Voices From the Dead*, you can be sure about Freemasonry, its doctrines and practices. You will have it from the Masonic authorities themselves.

Here, we will go direct to the experts—the highest level Masons, those who hold and held leadership positions as Sovereign Grand Commanders and have earned the coveted 33rd degree. For example, we will consult the book, *Morals and Dogma of the Ancient and Accepted Scottish Rite of Freemasonry*, written by none other then Albert Pike, 33°. The late Pike's cherished body is interned at the House of the Temple, the Scottish

Rite's international headquarters in Washington, D. C. What an honor! A statue erected in his honor sits on U.S. government-owned land in Judiciary Square of that same city. His 861-page book was for years given free to every man elevated to the third degree (Master Mason). It is found in every Masonic Lodge and every Masonic Lodge library in America.

Carl Claudy, another highly esteemed author on Freemasonry (*Introduction to Freemasonry, Volume 1, 2, and 3*), praised Albert Pike, writing about him: "Albert Pike is one of the greatest geniuses Freemasonry has ever known. He was a mystic a symbologist, a teacher of the hidden truths of Freemasonry."

Now wouldn't you like to read of Pike's great teachings on the doctrines of Freemasonry? We have them here in *Voices From the Dead*. His classic book was published in 1891, but you need not buy it (actually, I recommend that you do buy it, to confirm that *Voices From the Dead* reveals exactly what Pike taught on the "hidden truths of Freemasonry.")

Albert Pike is recognized perhaps as the greatest Masonic writer and thinker of all time. But not far behind is Manly P. Hall, 33°, whose many books on the Masonic Lodge are often quoted. Hall died in 1990, after publishing innumerable publications through his Philosophical Research Society in California. Among his classics is *The Secret Teachings of All Ages* (1977), a massive volume covering every aspect of the religion of Freemasonry and its dogma. Hall also penned the book, *Lectures on Ancient Philosophy*, (1984), as well as *The Lost Keys of Freemasonry* (1976) and *What the Ancient Wisdom*

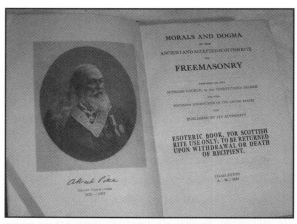

The front pages of Albert Pike's classic Masonic textbook, *Morals and Dogma*, is stamped: ESOTERIC BOOK FOR SCOTTISH RITE USE ONLY: TO BE RETURNED UPON WITHDRAWAL OR DEATH OF RECIPIENT.

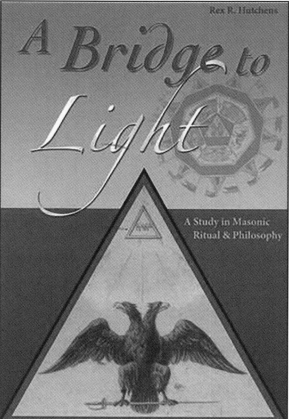

In 1988, the Scottish Rite (largest Masonic society on earth) published a condensed version of Pike's *Morals and Dogma*, entitled *A Bridge to Light*, by Rex Hutchens, 32°.

Expects of Its Disciples (1982).

Albert Pike is the man who actually originated today's 33-degree rituals of the Masonic Lodge. I am unable to find even one Mason who refutes or criticizes Pike's writings on the morals and doctrines of Freemasonry. He is author not only of the classic textbook, *Morals and Dogma*, but also authored a vast series of other books on Freemasonry.

In his book, *The House of the Temple of the Supreme Council*, C. Fred Kleinknecht, 33°, then the Sovereign Grand Commander of Scottish Rite Freemasonry, says of Pike: "Albert Pike remains today an inspiration for Masons everywhere. His great book, *Morals and Dogma*, endures as the most complete exposition of Scottish Rite Philosophy. He will always be remembered and revered as the "Master Builder of the Scottish Rite."

Pike's books are widely quoted by the highest authorities in Freemasonry today. His influence has only grown since his death in 1891. *Morals and Dogma* is published by the Supreme Council of the Scottish Rite of Freemasonry, Washington, D.C.

TWO

What Masonic Authorities, Dead and Alive, Teach

"There is in Christ's gospel a rapport with many religions: Christianity, Buddhism, Islam, Judaism, Brahmanism (Hinduism) and others. They originally arose from man's early fear of nature's forces. Gradual progress was made to higher and more mature concepts... Hence, there is an ultimate unanimity of belief that the great cause is the one God: that man is a partaker of divinity in that God dwells within him..."

—Henry C. Clausen, 33°
Sovereign Grand Commander,
Supreme Mother Council,
Emergence of the Mystical

W hat do Masonic authorities teach? I encourage you, dear friend, to read closely the above quote from a top Masonic leader. Do you see the gaping errors in Mr.

29

Clausen's statement? You and I know that Christ's gospel has *no* rapport with other religions. We know, too, that Christianity did not arise from "man's early fear of nature's forces," and certainly the Christian faith is not progressing to "more mature concepts." Most important, not every man has God dwelling "within him." Only born again Christian men and women have the Holy Spirit within.

Clausen's quote typifies what the Mason is taught inside the Lodge. Regrettably, it strays far from the truths given us in the Holy Bible.

I am privileged to provide you names of just a few of the many high-level Masonic authorities whose teaching and secrets you will find in this book. After reading their works, you will be prepared to debate any Mason in the world on the topic of Freemasonry. After all, *Voices From the Dead* quotes Masonic leaders, like Henry C. Clausen, 33°, recognized as superior in knowledge to virtually any Mason alive today.

Let them attempt to lie and obfuscate; sit back and observe as these Masons shrink and melt back into the landscape of their immoral and demonic religion. They cannot possibly deny all these fundamental sources of knowledge on the Masonic morality and doctrine. Here is the truth and nothing but the truth about the Masonic Lodge.

Parade to Glory, by Fred Van Deventer (Pyramid Books, New York, 1959)

A Bridge to Light, by Rex Hutchens, 32°, Mother

Supreme Council, Scottish Rite Freemasonry
(Washington, D.C., 1988)

Clausen's Commentaries on Morals and Dogma, by
Henry C. Clausen, 33°, Sovereign Grand Commander,
Scottish Rite Freemasonry (Washington, D.C., Mother
Supreme Council, 1976)

*Fire in the Minds of Men: Origins of the Revolutionary
Faith*, by James Billington, Executive Director of the
Library of Congress (Washington, D.C., Basic Books,
1980)

Introduction to Freemasonry, by Carl H. Claudy, 33°,
Three Volumes (Washington, D. C., Temple Publishers,
1931)

The Meaning of Masonry, by W. L. Wilmshurst, 33°
(New York, Bell Publishing, 1927)

The Spirit of Masonry, by Foster Bailey, 32° (London:
Lucis Trust, 1972)

*Blue Lodge Enlightenment: A Ritual of the Three
Masonic Degrees* (Chicago: Ezra Cook, 1964)

The Master's Book, by Carl Claudy, 33° (The Temple,
1985)

Practice and Procedure for the Scottish Rite, by Henry
C. Clausen, 33°, Sovereign Grand Commander
Washington, D.C. (The Supreme Council, 33rd Degree,

Mother Jurisdiction of the World, 1981)

*Funeral Ceremony and Offices of a Lodge of Sorrow of
the Ancient and Accepted Scottish Rite of Freemasonry*
(Charleston, S.C., 1946)

The Great Teaching of Masonry, by H. L. Haywood
(Richmond, V.A., Macoy, 1971)

Masonic World Guide, by Kent Henderson (Richmond,
V.A., Macoy, 1984)

A Comprehensive View of Freemasonry, by Henry
Wilson Coil (Richmond, V.A., Macoy, 1973)

*Liturgy of the Ancient and Accepted Scottish Rite of
Freemasonry for the Southern Jurisdiction of the United
States, Part 2*, by Albert Pike (Washington, D.C., The
Supreme Council, 33rd Degree, 1982)

*Mackey's Masonic Ritualist Monitorial Instructions and
the Degrees from Entered Apprentice to Select Masters*,
by Albert Pike (Charles E. Merrill, 1861)

*The Symbolism of Freemasonry: Illustrating and
Explaining Its Science and Philosophy, Its Legends,
Myths, and Symbols*, by Albert Mackey (Chicago:
Charles T. Powner Co., 1975)

Masonic Initiation, by W.L. Wilmshurst (Kila, Montana:
Kessinger Publishing)

The Builders, by Joseph Fort Newton, 33° (Richmond, V.A., Macoy, 1951)

The Craft and Its Symbols: Opening the Door to Masonic Symbolism, by Allan E. Roberts (Richmond, V.A., Macoy, 1974)

The Magnum Opus (or Great Work), by Albert Pike, 33° (Kessenger Publishing, Kila, Montana)

The Last Four Gathas of Zarathustra and Legends, by Albert Pike

Is It True What They Say About Freemasonry? by Art de Hoyos and S. Brent Morris, (Silver Springs, Maryland, the Masonic Service Association, 1994)

A Pilgrim's Path, by John Robinson (New York: M. Evans and Company, 1993)

An Encyclopedia of Freemasonry, by Albert G. Mackey, 33° (2 Volumes, New York: The Masonic History Company, 1873)

Royal Masonic Encyclopedia, by Kenneth Mackenzie (Wellingborough, Northhamptonshire, England, 1987)

Scottish Rite Masonry Illustrated (The Complete Ritual of the Ancient and Accepted Scottish Rite), by J. Blanchard (Chicago: Charles T. Powner, 1979)

Masonic Ritual and Monitor, by Malcolm C. Duncan

(New York: David McKay)

An Encyclopedic Outline of Masonic, Hermetic, Quabbalistic, and Rocicrucian Symbolic Philosophy, by Manly P. Hall (Los Angeles Philosophic Research Society, 1977)

Mackey's Revised Encyclopedia of Freemasonry (Three Volumes) Macoy, 1966)

Duncan's Ritual of Freemasonry, by Malcolm C. Duncan (David McKay Company)

A New Encyclopedia of Freemasonry, by Arthur E. Waite, 33° (New York: Weather Vane, 1970)

10,000 Famous Freemasons (Washington D.C., Mother Supreme Council, Scottish Rite Freemasons)

Coil's Masonic Encyclopedia, by Henry W. Coil, 33° (Macoy Publishers and Masonic Supply Company, 1961)

A Special Note to Masons

Now, what do the vast consensus of all these high Masonic authorities agree regarding their chosen brotherhood of Freemasonry? Read their books and encyclopedias closely and here is what you get:

> Freemasonry is a composite ancient Mystery religion involving the worship of Lucifer and inferior 'deities' through Jewish kabbalistic rituals and doctrine taught

by its Lodges and teachers.

Please notice, this description of the Masonic Order is essentially the same one that the many Christian researchers ascribe to, and it is the same that I have discovered in the many decades of research and investigation into New Age cults and religions (see *Texe Marrs Book of New Age Cults and Religions*).

So the highest authorities of Freemasonry—the men who have earned the 33rd degree, who have served as the Sovereign Grand Commanders of the Lodges and in other high positions and those who are acknowledged by the Mother Supreme Council of the Scottish Rite—all agree. Some, of course, deny the Masonic "Lucifer" connection. They might also quibble, say, on whether "Satan" is a real being or a symbol, or whether his name is "Lucifer" or Satan, but this is simply a sidebar. The fact is Masons of every degree, almost by consensus, agree that their "Great Architect" is not Jesus and that Freemasonry is a religion but is not Christianity.

I will admit that a few Masons might disagree with this description. After all one finds objectors and ignorant men everywhere, in every field today. I invite Masons to continue reading. If you truly want to know the facts about your own fraternity, you will find them here, in this book. Please don't be HOODWINKED.

THREE

My Wake-up Call Regarding Freemasonry

Voices From the Dead

*"Simeon Bar Yochai is at this 30th Degree ceremony.
In fact, he 'resides' over the entire ritual. He is the
'Voice from the Dead.'"*

Beginning in 1987, I authored a number of
Christian books which catapulted my
Ministry to high levels of visibility in the
Christian community. At the time, since my subjects
centered on the New Age movement, I had little
conception of the debate within Christianity regarding
Freemasonry. Yet I continued to be asked many questions
about Freemasonry; specifically, Christians wanted to
know if Freemasonry and Christianity were compatible.

The many questions caused me to spend considerable
time examining Freemasonry. In my examination, I
studied the textbooks of both Freemasonry and those

37

who opposed it. I had no bias whatsoever when I started my examination; the Masons I had met over the years seemed to be good people. Usually, they were stout members of the Community, men of high caliber.

But, Freemasonry itself was terribly lacking. It's precepts and doctrines clearly were not Christian in nature, and the name of Jesus Christ was prohibited during Masonic rituals and meetings. Not only that, but Freemasonry claimed to be a "religion" open to those of all other religions. Members could be Moslems, Jews, Buddhists, Zoroasters, or Jains. And the doctrines? These came not from Christianity but were admitted to have come from a "primitive universal religion."

Of course, Freemasonry violates the first of the Ten Commandments, *"Thou shalt have no other Gods before me."* What's more, no Christian man could join a "religion" that does not name and exalt Jesus Christ and He alone as Lord and Saviour.

Freemasonry, I discovered, is absolutely a pagan religious system incompatible with the Christian Church.

It was later, in 2015, however, when I received my real wake-up call regarding the absolute blasphemy and dangers of Freemasonry. While going over some old books, I came across the 3-volume set, *The Southern Baptist Convention and Freemasonry*. It was authored by my good friend, James L. Holly, a distinguished medical doctor practicing in Beaumont, Texas. I had read these volumes when they were first published, in 1992. Nevertheless, I picked *Volume 1* up and began reading it once again. That was when my eyes lighted on page 27, which quoted from Mackey's *Revised Encyclopedia of*

Freemasonry, volume 1, p. 166, from an article by Dr. Ginsburg entitled "Kabbalah."

The Masonic article recounts the miraculous story of a man, *Simeon Bar Yochai*, who lived in ancient Israel during the second century.

Somehow, I previously—back in 1992—had either overlooked or discounted the strange tale of Simeon Bar Yochai. Fortunately, in the intervening years I had spent many months studying the religion of Judaism and its divine worship of two famous sets of books—the *Babylonian Talmud* and the *Kabbalah*.

It turns out that this same man, Simeon Bar Yochai, is prominently mentioned by the rabbinical promoters of these books. *The Babylonian Talmud*, the book of sacred Jewish laws, shows this same man being often quoted. Yochai is a rabbi who is greatly honored by the Jews and his statements in the Talmud are *halacha* (or halakha); that is, the Law. We'll talk later about these laws.

It is the Kabbalah however, for which Simeon Bar Yochai is most well known. Jewish religious history records that Rabbi Simeon (or, Shimon) is the actual author of the Kabbalah, and thus chief of its five composite books, the *Zohar*.

So, Simeon Bar Yochai is an ancient rabbi whose words in the Talmud are considered law by today's Jews. He is the writer of the Kabbalah, the foundational source for the religion of Judaism. A famous man, indeed.

Please, pay close attention, because this man, this ancient rabbi, Simeon Bar Yochai, not only is famous for his Talmudic and Kabbalistic exploits, but also for his legendary role in Freemasonry, where he is at center stage in the ritual ceremony for the 30th Degree. He is the *"Voice of the Dead"* who greatly affects the lives and souls of millions of Freemasons. By following the words—and the Masonic oaths given to the 30th Degree candidates by Simeon Bar Yochai, the Masonic candidate consigns his soul to hell.

Could this be true? Could the words and acts of a Jewish rabbi who is, in simulation, brought back to life from the dead by today's Freemasonry, result in the hellish destiny of millions of today's Freemasons? We shall shortly see, for we will descend directly into the 30th Degree ceremony to reveal the part that the dead Rabbi Simeon Bar Yochai continues to play in the lives of many, almost totally unsuspecting, Freemasons

The 30° Ritual

The 30° is the Knight Kadosh Degree. "Kadosh" is the Hebrew word for "Holy." As we shall learn later in this book, all the 33 degree rituals are based on the Jewish Kabbalah. The Kabbalah is a system of black magic and sorcery from ancient Babylon underlying most cult and occult groups in the world.

The Kabbalah, Wilmshurst informs us in *The Meaning of Masonry*, is *"that marvelous system of secret, oral tradition of the Hebrews, a strong element of which has been introduced into our Masonic system."*

That "strong element" comes into clear focus in the 30° in which the candidate is told by the "Grand Pontiff" that he must engage in the *"Overthrow of all kinds of superstitions."* Thus, any dependence or belief in the sectarian faith of Christianity will be ended. He must accept that *all* religions are lower than Freemasonry, thus degrading Christianity, and he takes an oath to "restore to the Grand Architect of the Universe" (that is, to Lucifer!) his proper status as lord of all religions—all religions being the "maze of impostures."

Here is that oath given by the "Grand Pontiff" and taken for the 30th degree. It is one of four oaths taken for the 30° in which the candidate agrees and swears he will always defend Freemasonry and will work to "overthrow fanaticism, intolerance, imposture, and superstition." As Masonry makes known to the candidate in many of its degrees, this refers to *sectarian religion*, of which *Christianity* is only one (Freemasonry is proclaimed by the Masonic Lodge as a universalist Mystery religion that definitely is *not* Christianity).

First, prefatory to the oath, comes this explanation:

> "In all the preceding degrees you must have observed that the object of Scotch Masonry is to overthrow all kinds of superstitions, and that by admitting in her bosom on terms of the strictest equality, the members of all religions, of all creeds and all countries, without any distinction whatever, she has, and indeed can have, but one single object and that is to restore to the Grand Architect of the Universe, to the common father of the human race those who are lost in the maze of impostures, invented for the sole purpose of enslaving them. The Knights Kadosh recognize no particular religion, and for that reason we demand of you nothing more than to worship God. And whatever may be the religious forms imposed

upon you by superstition at a period of your life when you were incapable of discerning truth from falsehood, we do not even require you to relinquish them. Time and study alone can enlighten you. But remember that you will never be a true Mason unless you repudiate forever all superstitions and prejudices."

The candidate then takes the following oath:

"I, _____, solemnly and sincerely promise and swear wholly to devote myself to the emancipation of humanity; to practice toleration in political and religious matters especially, toward men. *To strive unceasingly* for the happiness of my fellow human beings, for the *propagation of light and or the overthrow of superstition, fanaticism, imposture, and intolerance.*"

The Grand Pontiff then instructs the candidate to toss some incense in the fire burning on the altar of perfumes while he prays the following:

"Almighty, Father Holy and Merciful. Oh! Thou of whom we are the beloved children, accept this incense which we offer thee with our hearts, as a token of love and reverence. *May thou kingdom come at last. And with it the end of all fanaticism, intolerance, imposture and superstition Amen.*"

After this, the candidate is instructed to write out a

confession of his belief in Masonry. After writing it, the confession is taken and will become a permanent record of the files of the Lodge.

And finally, the Knights Kadosh degree requires that the candidate be counseled as follows:

> "And finally, keep aloof from uniting yourself with any sectional, political, or sectarian religious organization whose principles can in any way bias your mind or judgement, or in the slightest degree trammel with obligations the vows you have just made."

In other words, he is told not to unite with any "sectarian religious organization" (Christianity included!) whose principles can bias his mind in the slightest degree from the obligation he has just taken. Christianity is out because if he is to be a solid Christian, he would willingly and proactively refuse to worship any other gods other than the God of the Bible. The book of *Philippians* tells us that the name of Jesus is above every other name. That certainly includes the ballyhooed "Great Architect of the Universe," whose real name of "God" is said to be *Ein Sof*. In reality the Masons and the Jews worship Lucifer—under these pretentious names.

The candidate for the 30th Degree is required by oath to refuse uniting with the religion of his childhood. He must cleave to Freemasonry's "primitive Mystery religion" and stay free of that "ignorant religion," the Christianity of his youth. This was made clear in his oath for the 28° ritual, known as the Knight of the Sun or Prince Adept Degree. In that degree ceremony, he was told:

"Many outsiders have the good fortune to enter our sanctuaries; but few indeed are fortunate enough to come to know the sublime truth (the secret they promise to reveal to him). If you ask what are the qualities a Mason must have to arrive at the center of true good it is necessary to have crushed the serpent of mundane ignorance; to have shaken off the yoke of the prejudices of childhood concerning the religion dominant in the country of his birth..."

The Masonic Lodge emphasizes in this degree, the 30th of 33, that Masons hate and despise "the religious and political rulers of this world." The Thrice Puissant Grand Master charges the candidate:

"Your assistance at this juncture is invaluable as we have crime to punish and innocence to protect. Persecution and oppression are raging. The religious and political rulers of the world will not render that justice which they have sworn to render, and we cannot endure their encroachments any longer."

Is the Lodge here talking about the famous and ancient Knights Templar, or, are they referring to the religions and rulers of today? We suspect the answer is both. For at this point, the Grand Master of the Lodge brings the candidate to a table on which he finds three *human skulls.* One skull wears a papal tiara, representing the unacceptable sectarian religions, the second wears a wreath of laurel, and the third skull wears a regal crown. The Grand Master stabs the first skull and the candidate angrily repeats, "Down with imposture! Down with crime!"

Both the Candidate and the Grand Master, then, kneel down before the skull which has the laurel wreath. This is the victorious Mason and is honored. Finally, the third skull is stabbed and the words said aloud, "Down with tyranny, Down with crime." Thus "government" is slain by the candidate.

Meeting with Satan—Simeon Bar Yochai

This book will shortly prove conclusively that Masonry is anti-Christian. It is not compatible with the Christian Church. But, what of Simeon Bar Yochai, the ancient rabbi? What part does he play in this blasphemous 30° ritual?

Rabbi Simeon Bar Yochai *is* at this 30th Degree ceremony. In fact, he "resides" over the entire ritual. He is the "Voice from the Dead." He speaks from his coffin.

FOUR

The Kadosh Knight Speaks From His Coffin

"Every Lodge is a Synagogue of Satan and its ritual is sorcery."
—Lady Queensborough
Occult Theocracy

"One is filled with admiration on penetrating into the Sanctuary of the Kabbalah, at seeing a doctrine, so simple, yet so absolute."
—Albert Pike, 33°
Morals and Dogma
(pp.744-745)

Possibly the one man who is most honored and revered in all of Freemasonry is Albert Pike, 33° (1809-1891), who created the 33 degree rituals. Masonic authority Carl Claudy, 33°, author of *Introduction to Freemasonry*, a 3-volume textbook set, wrote of Pike on page 105:

> "Albert Pike, one of the greatest geniuses Freemasonry has ever known. He was a mystic, a symbologist, a teacher of the hidden truth of Freemasonry."

Pike is so admired that his dead body is interred in a tomb at the Scottish Rite's international headquarters in Washington, D.C. The Masons even erected a statue of Pike on Judiciary Square in Washington, D. C. and there it still sits, even though Pike was a Confederate general and a convicted war criminal.

Pike was a student of Helena Blavatsky's Theosophy, a Judaic/Kabbalist religion, and a great admirer, as was Blavatsky, of the Kabbalah. Not only did he use its principles in designing the 33 ritual ceremonies, but its ideas, structure, and principles permeate Pike's Masonic textbook, *Morals and Dogma*.

Pike: Kabbalah Superior to the Holy Bible

In *Morals and Dogma*, Pike says that the Holy Bible is "incomplete and veiled," but the Kabbalah contains the "true secrets and traditional philosophy." Take a look at some of the beliefs of this Jewish Kabbalist, Albert Pike, as expressed in his book, *Morals and Dogma*:

> "All truly dogmatic religions have issued from the Kabalah and return to it. Everything scientific and grand in the religious dreams of all the illuminati,

Albert Pike, designer of the 33 ritual ceremonies.

Jacob Boehme, Swedenborg, Saint-Martin, and others, is borrowed from the Kabalah; all the Masonic associations owe to it their Secrets and their Symbols.

"The Kabalah alone consecrates the alliance of the Universal Reason and the Divine Word; it establishes, by the counterpoises of two forces apparently opposite, the eternal balance of being; it alone reconciles Reason with Faith, Power with Liberty, Science with Mystery; it has The keys of the Present, the Past, and the Future.

"The Bible, with all the allegories it contains, expresses, in an incomplete and veiled manner only, the religious science of the Hebrews. The doctrine of Moses and the Prophets, identical at bottom with that of the ancient Egyptians, also had its outward meaning and its veils. The Hebrew books were written only to recall to memory the traditions; and they were written in Symbols unintelligible to the Profane. The Pentateuch and the prophetic poems were merely elementary books of doctrine, morals, or lithurgy; and the true secret and traditional philosophy was only written afterward, under veils still less transparent. ` Thus was a second Bible born, unknown to, or rather uncomprehended by, the Christians; a collection, they say, of monstrous absurdities; a monument the adept says, wherein is everything that the genius of philosophy and that of religion have ever formed or imagined of the sublime; a treasure surrounded by thorns; a diamond concealed in a rough dark stone.

"One is filled with admiration, on penetrating into the Sanctuary of the Kabalah, at seeing a doctrine so logical so simple, and at the same time so absolute. The necessary union of ideas and signs, the consecration of the most fundamental realities by the primitive characters; the Trinity of Words, Letters, and

Numbers; a philosophy simple as the alphabet,
profound and infinite as the Word; theorems, more
complete and luminous than those of Pythagoras, a
theology summed up by counting on one's fingers;
and Infinite which can be held in the hollow of an
infant's hand; ten ciphers, and twenty-two letters, a
triangle, a square, and a circle,—these are all the
elements of the Kabalah. These are the elementary
principles of the written Word, reflection of that
spoken Word that created the world!

"This is the doctrine of Kabalah, with which you will
no doubt seek to make yourself acquainted, as to the
Creation."

Rabbi Bar Yochai Venerated and Honored by Pike

Being so enamoured of the Kabbalah that he holds it as
superior to the Holy Bible, and so impressed that he uses
its principles and teachings as models for all 33 degrees of
Freemasonry, making Masonry a kabbalist Mystery
religion, Pike greatly venerated and honored the *author*
of the Kabbalah. And, in fact, Masonry shows this is the
case.

The author of the Kabbalah is none other than *Rabbi
Simeon Bar Yochai*. And Albert Pike, in the pivotal 30° of
Freemasonry, showcases Yochai as a *Knight Kadosh*—that
is a "Holy Warrior." Yochai speaks from his coffin to the
30° Masonic candidates.

Charles David Hall, 33°, says that Freemasons hold
that the 30th Degree is "one of the most important." It
informs the Candidate of the "Lives of Great Men," the

A Jewish artist's conception of famous Rabbi Simeon Bar Yochai, second century author of the Kabbalah and its Zohar. Yochai, according to both the Jewish Encyclopedia and Wikipedia, is described as the "pre-eminant anti-Gentile teacher." He is quoted in the Talmud as saying, "The best of the gentiles—kill!" His kabbalistic works are the basis for the doctrines of Freemasonry. He is honored in Freemasonry's 30th Degree, the Knight of Kadosh.

most pre-eminent being Rabbi Simeon Bar Yochai.

Let's review this key part of the 30° ritual ceremony, as reported by Dr. James L. Holly, in his 1992 book, *The Southern Baptist Convention and Freemasonry* (The ritual descriptions in Holly's book are from the book, *Scottish Rite Masonry Illustrated* (Powner Company, Chicago, Illinois) and the story of Rabbi Simeon Bar Yochai is from *The Encyclopedia of Freemasonry*, by Albert Mackey, 33°).

Simeon Bar Yochai—The Dead Man in the Coffin

In the initiatory ritual of the thirtieth degree there are four apartments or rooms with special decorations which symbolize different aspects of the occult. In this degree, there are four oaths that are recited. In the first apartment the following furnishings are present:

> "This apartment is hung with black tapestry. A sepulchral lamp is suspended from the vault. In the middle is a mausoleum, above which is a coffin. In the coffin lies a knight, wrapped up in a white shroud, his face veiled. On the platform of the mausoleum are three skulls... At the west end of the apartment is a large transparency on which are written in flame colored letters the following words: 'Whoever shall overcome the dread of death, shall

This eerie scene is a painting of part of the 30th degree ritual of Freemasonry. Painted by Jo Whaley of Santa Fe, New Mexico, the painting shows the catacomb-like interior of the Lodge and three strange figures wearing black robes and hoods. On the altar at right are three skulls.

emerge from the bosom of the earth, and have a
right to be initiated into the greater mysteries.'"
(Scotch Rite Masonry Illustrated, p. 257)

That the above does not describe the ornaments of a
Christian service needs no argument. That it does involve
the occultic and Luciferianism is obvious. The initiate is
about to recognize that he has become an illuminati in the
Kaballa faith which Scripture condemns.

"My brother, these objects conceal a great mystery.
Are you prepared to undergo the trials which await
you? They are fearful but there is nothing in them to
alarm you if you have understood the degrees
through which you have successively passed. I warn
you moreover, that you will have to answer very
serious questions, and must advise you to confine
yourself in all your answers to these words only, 'I
wish to proceed.' You must collect all of your power
of your mind, for on yourself alone you will have to
depend." (Ibid, p. 258)

The Thrice Puissant Grand Master admits that even though
the real meaning of the Masonic symbols are concealed
from the men of the lower degrees, that "if you have
understood," then you will already know what you are
about to be told. The occultism of the Lodge is discernable
at the lower degrees if a man is listening. The lies of
Freemasonry, withheld from the Blue lodge members, are
contained in the symbolism of those lower degrees, if a
person is able to discern them. All men of the Lodge are

without excuse. Either they are lost and blind, or they have allowed Satan to blind them.

Secondly, and more diabolical is the statement "for on yourself alone you will have to depend." The Christian God has said "I will never leave you nor forsake you." Where is this God who promised such? Why are "Christians" encouraged to cast Him aside and to rely only upon themselves? Why must the Christian be stripped of the reality of the Presence of the True God in order to proceed in this "brotherhood"? The reason becomes apparent soon.

The Dead Man in the Coffin Speaks Again

Once again, the words of the Knight in the coffin are heard, but this time with the identity of the interrogator and with the understanding of what he intends:

> "Thou who comest hither to disturb my rest fear my wrath. What is thy wish?" (*Scottish Rite Masonry Illustrated, Volume II*, p. 259)

The initiate, on his own now, answers as he was instructed, "I wish to proceed." So the initiate, unknowingly perhaps, but nonetheless certainly, begins his fatal converse with the enemy of his soul. After a moment the ceremony continues.

> "The door is thrown open with a fearful crash. The Knight in the coffin resumes his position. Thrice Puissant Grand Master enters the room hurriedly with a burning torch in his left hand and a dirk raised in his right. The music stops. He walks up to

This Masonic drawing symbolizes Rabbi Bar Yochai as he speaks to the 30th degree candidate from his coffin.

the candidate and says to him in a threatening voice:

'Since your wish is to proceed; since your rashness prompts you to dare the wrath in store for so many centuries follow me.'" (Ibid, p. 259)

The Thrice Puissant Grand Master then walking up majestically to the mausoleum and kneeling before the skull wreathed with the laurel says, "Kneel down with me." He continues:

"Hitherto you have seen in masonry nothing but emblems and symbols. Now you must see in it nothing but reality.- Are you determined to repudiate all prejudices and to obey, without reserve all that you will be commanded to do for the good of humanity?" (Ibid, p. 259)

Innocent enough it may seem on the surface. But the reality of the symbols to be seen is Luciferianism and the prejudices to be repudiated are Christian doctrine and the unique revelation of God in Jesus Christ. The greatest problem in the church today, beyond unbelief, is rebellion. Here it is seen that even Lucifer knows of the need for obedience and submission.

Secret Worship Paid to Simeon Bar Yochai

In his article, "Ancient Mysteries" in his *Encyclopedia of Freemasonry* (Vol. 2), Albert Mackey notes the "special worship" paid in the Mysteries to the pagan gods:

"Each of the pagan gods had besides the public and open a secret worship paid to him to which none were admitted but those who had been selected by prepratory ceremonies called Initiation. This secret worship was termed the Mysteries."

It seems feasible, then, that Pike and higher level Masons pay a "special worship" to Simeon Bar Yochai. He is, after all, the "Father of their Mystery Religion,

Freemasonry," for it is based on his book, the *Kabbalah*, and especially on the *Zohar*, a component of the Kabbalah. Recognizing him in the 30° is one form of this "secret worship." It is sure that few Masons being initiated know who Simeon Bar Yochai is. They are not told in the ceremony that he authored the Kabbalah from which comes their religion of Freemasonry. Albert Pike gives the Candidates a big clue to his identity when he states that he will uncover "the Mystery of the Kabbalah." But the Candidate knows him only as the Voice from the Dead, who speaks from his coffin to them; he is the Knight Kadosh, the "Holy Warrior."

Simeon Bar Yochai—The Rabbi Who Despised and Hated Christianity

But Albert Pike, the acknowledged hero and author of the rituals, well knows of this Simeon Bar Yochai. *He is the ancient rabbi who is said to be the most devoted and fiercest opponent of Christianity. He despised Christians and taught that every Christian should be put to death!*
Yochai's conclusions about Christians are not only found in the Kabbalah, but are the *law* of the Talmud:

> "The best of the Christians—Kill!"
>   (Yer. Kid. iv. 66cl Massek Soferiar xv 10;
>   comp. Mek., Beshallah, Wayehi, 1, and
>   Tan., Wayera 20)

This Jewish law is repeated in the *Jewish Encyclopedia*, which reports that this was only one indication of Yochai's "animosity toward the Gentiles." Yochai is also quoted in the *Encyclopedia* as calling Gentiles "*Serpents:*"

"The best of Serpents should have its head crushed."

As to women, the *Encyclopedia* says that Rabbi Simeon Bar Yochai generally is hostile to women, as is true of all orthodox Jews. Of women, Yochai is reported to have said that, "the most pious of women is prone to sorcery."

One wonders if this hostility toward women is the reason why Freemasonry has always excluded women from its membership ranks. The same discrimination is applied toward Africans (blacks), and this bigotry has encouraged blacks to establish their own form of Masonry—the Prince Hall Masons.

Hatred of Christians—and of Christianity

How many lower-level Freemasons know that when they progress upward to reach the exalted 30° they will meet this "Voice from the Dead—Rabbi Simeon Bar Yochai?" Are they not being hoodwinked, deceived, all the way to perdition?

Think of it—the average Mason, upon vying for the 30°, responds to the dead Rabbi's voice. He proclaims, "*I wish to proceed.*" And so he does, renouncing his Christian faith, agreeing that Jesus become subordinate to Masonry, and that Christianity and all other religions are mere "fanaticism and superstition."

Would the 30° candidate take this deadly oath if he knew in advance that the Voice from the Dead, this "Holy Warrior," was that of the ancient rabbi who so

The tomb of Rabbi Simeon Bar Yochai is a popular tourist attraction in Israel today. Millions visit the tomb each year.

A painting depicting the famous Rabbi Simeon Bar Yochai who supposedly spent twelve years deep in a cave writing the occultic textbook, the *Zohar*, central to today's Kabbalah of Judaism.

The body of Rabbi Bar Yochai is honored inside his tomb.

hated Christians and Gentiles he had said—and it is today Jewish law in their Talmud:

"The best of the Christians—kill!"

Would he say, "I wish to proceed," knowing this horrible rabbi is the one who invented the *Zohar*, with its many exhibitions of grotesque black magic, its foul sorcery, its multiplicity of gods and goddesses and its literal worship of the Holy Serpent (Lucifer)!

What a cruel and massive deception is this terrible hoax being played out against the unsuspecting Mason!

Pedophilia in the Talmud—Brought to You by Rabbi Simeon Bar Yochai

Here is what we have so far discovered, that:

1. Albert Pike, the "Father" of modern Masonry, fully endorses the Jewish Kabbalah, claiming it is the one source of truth, superior to the Holy Bible.

2. Rabbi Simeon Bar Yochai is the author of the Jewish Kabbalah and its chief volume, the *Book of Zohar*.

3. Rabbi Simeon Bar Yochai is honored in Freemasonry as the Voice From the Dead, speaking to the 30° candidate from his coffin.

4. This is the same Rabbi Bar Yochai who is quoted in the Talmud: "The best of the Christians—kill!"

But, there is more! My research indicates that Yochai is one of the most honored rabbis in Judaism *today*, and he is author of the notorious Talmud law that says that pedophilia, that is, intercourse sex, is permissible with a 3-year old little girl. In fact, Bar Yochai says in the Talmud that a Jewish Priest may take a 3-year old to be his bride!

Here is a recent, edited article about this atrocity, as reported by the Reverend Theodore Pike of *The National Prayer Network*, entitled, "Judaism's Pedophilia Begins with Rabbi Ben Yochai" (Sept. 25, 2013).

Judaism's Pedophilia Begins with Rabbi Bar Yochai

Yeshiva University in New York City is the latest Jewish educational institution to be rocked by accusations of extensive pedophilia by rabbis and teachers. Yeshiva, including an elite high school, the Albert Einstein College of Medicine, the Benjamin N. Cardoza School of Law, and an endowment of nearly 1.3 billion dollars, is the Harvard of Orthodox Judaism in America. But now 31 former high school and Yeshiva affiliate students allege sexual abuse by two highly respected Yeshiva rabbis during 1969-1989, They are suing Yeshiva U. for 380 million dollars. "Yeshiva University High School held itself out as an exemplary Jewish secondary school when in fact it was allowing known sexual predators to roam the school at will seeking other victims," said attorney for the plaintiffs, Kevin Mulhearn. Mulhearn asserts that hundreds of boys were sexually molested or sodomized.

Typically, as with other Jewish child abuse scandals in Brooklyn, Sydney, Melbourne, Jerusalem, etc., Yeshiva's administration is evasive.

Why do Jewish authority figures continue to be accused of pedophilia against primarily Jewish children? The Talmud, highest authority for modern Talmudic Judaism, endorses pedophilia. It calls it "Halachah" or binding Jewish law!

The Talmudic rabbi most instrumental in persuading rabbis today to indulge in pedophilia is 2nd century A.D. Simeon Bar Yochai. It's hard to imagine a rabbinic sage more esteemed than Bar Yochai. He is credited by Ultra-Orthodox Jews as the author of the Zohar, or Kabbalah. Every year in Meron in Israel (where Bar Yochai died), more than 10,000 Hasidic Jews gather for a week of singing, dancing, and praising Yochai, who may well be Kabbalist Judaism's most venerated authority.

In Orthodox Judaism, the most ancient first and second AD rabbis, the "Tannaim," are considered most authoritative. This is largely because they lived in Palestine closest in time to the Pharisees who, originating in Babylon, created the Mishnah (oral law), which later became written down as the Babylonian Talmud. Some "Tanna" receive greater respect from Orthodox Jews than does Moses. Jesus accused the oral law of "making the law of God of none effect."

The Talmud is the greatest religious authority for observant Jews today. Thus, when Yochai authorizes pedophilia in the Talmud, such permission becomes law for Orthodox Jews for all time.

In Yebamoth 6ob the Talmud says:

"It was taught: R. Simeon Bar Yochai stated: 'proselyte who is under the age of three years and

one day is permitted to marry a priest. For it is said,
But all the women children that have not known
men by lying with them, keep for yourselves; and
Phinehas surely was with them.'"

Bar Yochai's interpretation comes from Numbers 31:18.
The Hebrews, after defeating the Midianites, were allowed
to keep virginal females of all ages as wives or potential
wives when they sexually matured. Bar Yochai exploited this
verse to claim God gives Jews rights to sexual use of
females of virtually any age, although he puts the lower bar
at three years and a day. Further, he says that because the
righteous Phinehas was among the Hebrew congregation
who accepted the Midianite women, it means that Phinehas
endorsed child sex.

Footnote 5 to this passage says Yochai's permission for
sex with 3-year-old girls stands for all time. The footnote
asks "How could they (any other rabbi in history), contrary
to the opinions of R. Simeon Bar Yochai, which has scriptural
support, forbid the marriage of the young proselytes?"
Clearly, they can't. (The full text of this footnote and the
entire passage from the Soncino edition of the Talmud are
at the end of Theodore Pike's article).

Thus, the question posed by the Talmud footnote is
extremely significant and timely. It says that just as no
rabbinic authority can defy Yochai's halachic permission for
sex with 3-year-old girls, so no rabbinic authority in any
Jewish organization, synagogue, Yeshiva high school,
college, or seminary today is empowered to declare that
pedophilia for the Jew is wrong!

Of course, Jewish leaders and rabbinic councils do

vocally condemn pedophilia while embroiled in scandal. But that is in order that, as the Talmud commands, "the name of God be not profaned" by bringing a bad reputation to Judaism."

But if an Orthodox rabbi believes anything, it is that every letter of the Talmud is divinely inspired. If it is necessary to lie about its contents, then the Talmud encourages such subterfuge, saying "it is permitted to deceive a goy" (gentile). (Baba Kama 113b)

Is the Man in the Coffin Rabbi Simeon Bar Yochai, or is He Satan in Disguise?

James L. Holly, MD, the astute Christian author of *The Southern Baptist Convention and Freemasonry*, asks this probing question:

> "Who was Simeon Bar Yohai (or, "Yochai")? He was the one and same as in Isaiah 14:16, He was Lucifer or one of his demons disguised in the form of a man. Who does the man in the coffin in the thirtieth degree represent? He is Lucifer himself or one of his demons."

Simeon Bar Yochai, the Voice from the Dead in the 30th Degree, may well be Lucifer himself. There are many legends—what the Apostle Paul called "Jewish fables"—in Orthodox Judaism. The Kabbalah is full of improbable magic, sorcery, and legends. The Bible notes that Satan, or Lucifer, often comes as an "Angel of Light" and his demonic agents as "Ministers of Righteousness."

Indeed, the Deity of Freemasonry, whom they title the Grand Architect of the Universe, is clearly the god, or deity of the Kabbalah. He is identified in the various Masonic rituals as Mahabone, Abaddon, and as Jahbulon. But in the Kabbalah, this Deity is known as *Ein Sof* and it is Lucifer, as the Holy Serpent, who is claimed to be man's "companion and helper." Who exactly is this mysterious Deity of the Kabbalah known as *Ein Sof*? Albert Mackey, in his *Encyclopedia of Freemasonry* (p. 167) says that he's known among kabbalists:

> "This is he who causes the earth to quake and kingdoms to shake."

Thus, Dr. Holly notes that Ein Sof is found in the Holy Bible, where his name is identified as none other than Lucifer. *Isaiah 14:16* reveals of Lucifer:

> "They that see thee shall narrowly look upon thee, and consider thee, saying is this the man that makes the earth to tremble, that did shake kingdoms..."

We find, then, an astonishing and revealing correspondence between the Kabbalah, whose strange God is Ein Sof, and the Holy Bible, which identifies Lucifer. *Ein Sof is Lucifer!*

Is this the "Mystery of the Kabbalah" promised to be revealed to Masons in the 30° ritual by Albert Pike, that their Deity is none other than Lucifer, *"he who causes the earth to quake and kingdoms to shake?"*

Similarities Between Yochai and Lucifer

The similarities between Simeon Bar Yochai in Freemasonry and Lucifer are striking. In Mackey's *Revised Encyclopedia of Freemasonry*, it reads:

> "When the rabbi died, kabbalists believe that a *dazzling light* filled the coffin..."

We recall that Pike describes Lucifer as the "source of light" and as the "Light Bearer." The Apostle Paul tells us that, *"Satan himself is transformed into an angel of light"* (2 Corinthians 11:14).

In the 30th Degree drama, the Lodge is transformed into a place of the dead. Drapes are black, human skulls are observed, candles are lit, and there, in a coffin, lies the mysterious Knight Kadosh. In the Kabbalah, and in Mackey's *Encyclopedia* we are told that when Simeon Bar Yochai died, his remains were deposited deep down a cave where a rocky tomb was prepared:

> "and when the remains were deposited in the tomb, another voice was heard from heaven, saying, 'This is he who caused the earth to shake and the kingdoms to shake.'"

That, of course, according to *Isaiah 14:12*, would be Lucifer, as Dr. Holly notes. Are Bar Yochai and Lucifer the same personage? Certainly, there are many instances of Satan's spirit (or that of one of his demons) entering a possessed man. This may well have been the case with Simeon Bar Yochai.

The Evidence for Demons in Masonry

The evidence of dark angels—which we know of as demons—and demon possession in Freemasonry is strong, and we hear of it from the testimony of Masons themselves. The quote below comes from the book, *The Hidden Life in Freemasonry*, authored by 33rd degree Mason, C. W. Leadbeater:

> "The 30th degree brings its angel also...who lends his strength to the Knight...the 33rd degree links the Sovereign Grand Inspector General with the spiritual King of the World Himself—that mightiest of Adepts... in whose strong hands is the destinies of earth...
>
> "Yet, when one of these bright spirits is attached to us by a Masonic ceremony we must not think of him either as a director or as an attendant but simply as a co-worker and brother."

Masons Are Alarmed by Holly's Disclosure of the Knight in the Coffin

It seems that Dr. Holly's writings regarding Bar Yochai and his role as the Knight in the Coffin during the 30° ritual alarmed many Freemasons. Moreover, Holly's astute observation that Yochai is actually "Satan" in disguise delivered a further shock to Freemasonry and its top officials. This secret had been hush hush for many decades, and lower-level Masons had been kept in the dark. Now, many would discover the identity of the "Voice From the Dead" that motivates the 30th Degree Candidate to ditch his native religion of Christianity and, instead, embrace the kabbalist doctrines of the Masonic Mystery religion.

Freemasonry immediately attempted damage control. One of the fraternity's chief apologists, John Robinson, 32°, came forth with commentary in his book, *A Pilgrim's Path* (M. Evans & Company, 1993), attempting to downplay Holly's revealing statements. Unfortunately, Mr. Robinson merely made things worse for Masonry. He wrote:

> "In the chambers prepared for the drama of the 30th degree there is a knight in a coffin... Dr. Holly asks, who does the knight in the coffin represent? Albert Pike says that the answer lies in the mystery of the Kabbalah."

Then, quite frankly admitting that the Knight in the coffin does, in fact, represent Rabbi Simeon Bar Yochai, Robinson quickly interjects some nonsense about how wonderful a man was the historic Rabbi Bar Yochai. Robinson claims that in the 30th Degree, *"Simeon Bar Yochai is presented as a man who has found favor with God."*

What a stretch! Is Robinson totally unaware that Rabbi Simeon Bar Yochai is infamous for his talmudic prescription, *"The best of the Christians—kill!"* Did this find the violent rabbi "favor with God?" This is the rabbi praised by today's Jewish authorities for his extremist views and abiding animosity toward Jesus Christ and Christianity. Yochai is known as a hater of both Gentiles and Christians.

Robinson must feel that he can easily hoodwink and
deceive his Masonic brethren, few of whom are aware of
the hateful role played by Rabbi Simeon Bar Yochai
toward Christianity.

Robinson next attempts to cast Yochai in a morbidly
sympathetic Christian light. He suggests that:

> "There are some who feel that he (Simeon Bar Yochai)
> symbolizes all of the Christians who died at the hands
> of their persecuters."

Unbelievable! In fact, Rabbi Bar Yochai *led* violent
attacks on Christians. According to Jewish history, he also
fought the Roman authorities and was forced to flee and
hid deep down a rocky cave for 12 years. It was during
this period, it is claimed, that Yochai wrote the infamous
Kabbalah and its satanic *Zohar*. That Robinson would
suggest today that this hateful and bigoted rabbi who so
hated and reviled Gentiles and Christians would, as a
Knight Kadosh in Freemasonry ("Holy Warrior"),
symbolize all of the Christians who died at the hands of
their persecutors is preposterous.

Robinson's false claims in his book proves the
desperation of Masonry. They do not want Masonry's
hoodwinked masses to know of their incredulous support
for the rabbi who both hated Christians and, at the same
time, sanctioned pedophile sex with three-year old girls.

The Kabbalah of Judaism and Freemasonry

"The Kabbalah teaches that the Holy Serpent is the Messiah...and the Great Secret is that the Serpent is, in fact, the 'God' of the Jews."

Since Freemasonry claims to be a primitive Mystery religion based on the Kabbalah, let us touch on the Kabbalah. First, the "God" or "Deity" of the Kabbalah is claimed to be named Ein Sof (or Ain Sof). Actually, the Jews say he has no name. Albert Pike, in *Morals and Dogma* explains:

> "The Absolute Deity, with the Kabalists, has no name. The terms applied to Him are אזד פשזם, AOR PASOT, the Most Simple (or Pure) Light, called איך מזף, AYEN SOPH, or INFINITE, before any Emanation. For then there was no space or vacant place, but all was infinite Light."

"Before the Deity created any Ideal, any limited and intelligible Nature, or any form whatever, He was alone, and without form or similitude, and there could be no cognition or comprehension of Him in any wise. He was without Idea or Figure, and it is forbidden to form any Idea or Figure of Him, neither by the letter He (ה), nor by the letter Yōd (י), though these are contained in the Holy name; nor by any other letter or point in the world."

The Deity is only identified as the vague and mysterious Grand Architect of the Universe in Freemasonry. According to the Kabbalah the Deity has no name. He is not a personal God, has no form, and cannot be communicated with (you can't pray to Him!). His is the "Light of the Infinite" and from him came "sparks of light." These sparks populate the earth and the universe and are separate gods, goddesses, and other deities and magical intelligences. These sparks exist in separate universes and are called the *Sephiroth*. There are generally ten different Sephiroth in the Tree of Life, some good and some evil.

The Kabbalah claims there is a Mother Goddess (spark or Sephiroth) and a Daughter Goddess, a Father God and a Son God. There is also a deity or spark called Yesod. Yesod is a phallus deity and has sex with the Daughter Goddess whose name is Malkuth (see opposite page for chart of the Kabbalistic Tree of Life). At the top of this Tree of Life is Kether, the Crown Goddess. But unseen and beyond Kether is Ein Sof, unseen and unable to communicate with men.

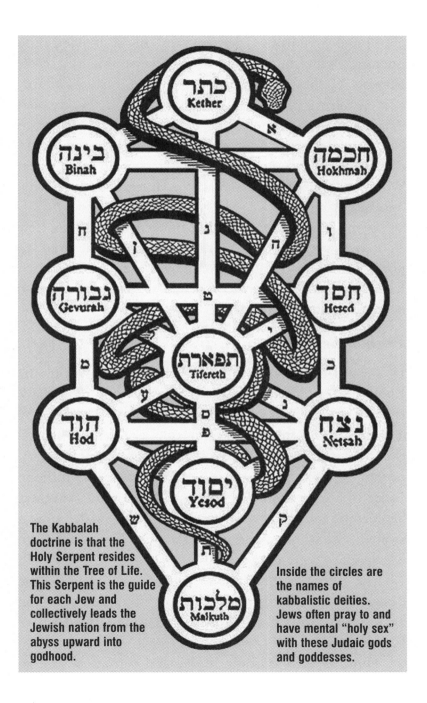

The Kabbalah doctrine is that the Holy Serpent resides within the Tree of Life. This Serpent is the guide for each Jew and collectively leads the Jewish nation from the abyss upward into godhood.

Inside the circles are the names of kabbalistic deities. Jews often pray to and have mental "holy sex" with these Judaic gods and goddesses.

These Sephiroth (deities) are all controlled and operated with the help of their companion, the Holy Serpent. He has sex with the female Sephiroth. The Holy Serpent also is the Agent of Help for man. He assisted Adam and Eve in the Garden, positively advising them to eat of the forbidden fruit and facilitating their pathway to divinity. Likewise, he helps men, facilitating their Great Work as they strive to reach perfection and become "gods."

Eventually, all enlightened men (Jews and a few righteous pro-Zionism Gentiles) will be elevated to godhood. The Holy Serpent will be the Messiah-facilitator, helping men to become as gods. Men are to become their own messiahs.

Freemasonry Has Been Deceived

It is easy to see why Pike and the Masons adore the Kabbalah. Its doctrines make men into gods. They have no reason to obey the kabbalistic version of "God" for he is impersonal, is mute, and cannot be reached. His sparks, the Sephiroth, however can be communicated with, prayed to, and man is able to have mental sex with them. Indeed via sex, mental sex with the Mother and Daughter Sephiroth and by proxy here on earth with human women, the whole world is regenerated. Thus, kabbalism is essentially a sex cult.

The ages-old heresy is what Freemasonry is—the desire to be one's own god and the attempted rebellion against the God of the Bible. That is the awful sin of Freemasonry.

Thus, as one Masonic leader and former Sovereign

Grand Commander emphasized, *"We must return to a faith in man himself."*

Another Masonic leader and writer, Wilmshurst, explained that Freemasons would reveal to man *"the ultimate divinity at the base of human nature."*

Albert Pike's grandiose scheme is shared by many in Freemasonry. He sought a Freemasonry rule of the world:

> "The World will soon come to us for its Sovereigns and Pontiffs. We shall constitute the equilibrium of the universe and be rulers over the Masters of the world."
> —Albert Pike,
> *Morals and Dogma*, p. 817

> "...Freedom marches ever onward toward the conquest of the world."
> —Albert Pike, *Legenda*, p.160 as quoted in
> *A Bridge to Light*, p. 291

> "Such, my Brother, is the TRUE WORD OF A MASTER MASON, such the true ROYAL SECRET, which makes possible, and shall at length make real, the HOLY EMPIRE of true Masonic Brotherhood."
> —Albert Pike
> *A Bridge to Light*, p. 325

A Jewish Professor Who Opposes Kabbalism Explains It

Israel Shahak, who passed away in 2001, was a decided opponent of kabbalism which he saw as poisonous and a great detriment to the Jewish people. Shahak, a professor at Hebrew University in Israel, wrote several excellent books about the Kabbalah and its practice.

He noted first that over the past 200 years, the Kabbalah has gained a dominant hold on the religion of Judaism. Yet, Shahak wrote that kabbalism is *not* classic Judaism but is an occult variant more like Hinduism, the religion of ancient Egypt, or the religions of ancient Greece and Rome.

Second, Professor Shahak says the misconception among Christians and non-Jews that Judaism today is a monotheistic worship of a religion is simply not true. He also emphasizes that Judaism today does not honor either the Old Testament or the New Testament. These components of the Holy Bible do not have in the Jewish religion the "same central place and legal authority which the Bible has for Protestant or even Catholic Christianity."

Judaism, he says, is based on the teachings of mysticism which developed in the 12th and 13th centuries and is today known as "kabbalism."

Below is a brief description Dr. Shahak provides the readers on the structure and beliefs of Judaic kabbalism:

> "According to the cabbala, the universe is ruled not by one god but by several deities, of various characters and influences, emanated by a dim, distant First Cause. Omitting many details, one can summarize the system as follows. From the First Cause, first a male god called 'Wisdom' or 'Father' and then a female goddess called 'Knowledge' or 'Mother' were emanated or born. From the marriage of these two, a pair of younger gods were born: Son, also called by many other names such as 'Small Face' or 'The Holy

Blessed One': and Daughter, also called 'Lady' (or 'Matronit', a word derived from Latin). 'Shekhinah', 'Queen', and so on.

"These two younger gods should be united, but their union is prevented by the machinations of Satan, who in this system is a very important and independent personage. The Creation was undertaken by the First Case in order to allow them to unite, but because of the Fall they became more disunited than ever, and indeed Satan has managed to come very close to the divine Daughter and even to rape her (either seemingly or in fact—opinions differ on this). The creation of the Jewish people was undertaken in order to mend the break caused by Adam and Eve, and under Mount Sinai this was for a moment achieved: the male god son, incarnated in Moses was united with the goddess Shekhinah. Unfortunately, the sin of the Golden Calf again caused disunity in the godhead; but the repentance of the Jewish people has mended matters to some extent.

"Similarly, each incident of biblical Jewish history is believed to be associated with the union or disunion of the divine pair. Daughter falls closely into the power of Satan, while Son takes various female satanic personages to his bed, instead of his proper wife.

"The duty of pious Jews is to restore through their prayers and religious acts the perfect divine unity, in

the form of sexual union, between the male and
female deities."

A Further Primer on the Kabbalah

In studying the New Age movement, I continually came
across a series of books related to the *Kabbalah*. These
books were prominently displayed on the shelves of New
Age bookstores. I bought most of the books on *Kabbalah*
and quickly realized that they were part and parcel of the
New Age. I also discovered that the *Kabbalah* was
extremely important to Judaism.

Moreover, I learned that Judaism has little to do with
the Old Testament. Rabbinical Seminaries—called
Yeshivas—pay little or no attention to the Old Testament.
The majority of their studies have to do with the
Babylonian Talmud, the Jews' books (actually some 68
volumes) of 613 laws and commentaries.

In the Talmud are many teachings of the Kabbalah.
And most rabbis combine both the Talmud and the
Kabbalah to round out their Jewish theological education.

This means, of course, that Judaism, infused with
teachings of the Kabbalah and the Talmud, is occultic and
New Age to its very core.

Given this inescapable connection, I have now spent
almost 30 years studying both the Talmud and the
Kabbalah, contrasting these foundational books of
Judaism with the doctrines and beliefs of New Age cults
and religions. Here are the facts regarding my research:

- Judaism is a rabbinical cult. It is not based on
  revelation but on a combination of skewed human

reason and rampant human fantasy. Both the Talmud and the Kabbalah are authored by biased Jewish rabbis who have rejected the truth of Jesus Christ.

- While the Talmud does have 613 laws and the Jew must attempt to navigate through all of these very petty and often silly rules, Judaism is not centered on the rigid Talmud but, instead, on the imaginative and fantastical books of the Kabbalah.

- The Kabbalah is at the very heart of Judaism. It grips the religious Jew with its bizarre doctrinal structure and introduces a fascinating array of mystical, magical practices to occupy his mind and his energy.

- These mystical magical practices of the Kabbalah include gematria (the magic of numerology), astrology, necromancy (communicating with dead spirits), color mysticism, chanting, mantras, dream interpretation, astral travel, goddess worship, sexual tantra, occult visualization, divination, occult symbolism, altered states of consciousness, psychic mind powers, idol worship, and other elements of witchcraft.

The *Kabbalah* is derived from the Mystery Religions of Babylon, Persia, Sumeria, Egypt, Greece, Rome, and other pagan cultures. The rabbis simply borrowed from these ancient writings. This is the reason for its similarity to other New Age cults and religions, which are also based on Mystery Teachings.

Both the Talmud and the Kabbalah are racist

documents. Both hold the conscious Jew as the ultimate in evolution and as gods on earth. Gentiles are but cattle and the Jews, as sparks of God, are destined to rule.

The Kabbalah greatly expands the Talmud's concept of "God." The Kabbalah teaches of many minor gods and goddesses, including ten emanations of the unknowable, unapproachable supreme "God." Moreover, "God" has a wife, a Holy Presence known as "Shekhinah."

The Kabbalah is essentially a lewd guide for a mind-sick sex cult. One of the deities in the Kabbalah's Tree of Life is Yesod, the phallus! Yesod continually lusts after and has sex frequently with Malkuth, a goddess. Plus, a higher feminine deity, the goddess Binah, has sex with yet another god, Tiphereth. Satan, meanwhile enjoys sex with both Binah and Malkuth, and with lesser personages of the multifaceted Jewish godhead. Meanwhile, Jewish persons here on earth copulate believing they are fostering frequent sex in the heavenlies by the gods and goddesses. *Judaism is a weird, lustful religion complete with human-god swingers and wild and frequent sex!* Even incestuous relations are encouraged among the gods and goddesses.

- The Kabbalah teaches that God encloses the universe within himself, that the Holy Serpent, named Leviathian, is the "Angel of help" that shall lift the Jew to rulership on Planet Earth, and that Jews must do both evil and good works to ascend to godhood. God, then, is Himself both good and evil, a combination of both the darkness and light.

- The Kabbalah teaches that the Holy Serpent is the

Messiah of the Jews and the Great Secret is that the Serpent, is, in fact, the "God" of the Jews. As such, he is depicted as enclosing the entire universe inside himself as the Ouroboros, the eternal Serpent biting its own tail.

Pike, Freemasonry, Rabbi Simeon Bar Yochai, and the Holy Serpent

Now we return again to Albert Pike, founder of modern Masonry and its 33 ritual degrees, and to Rabbi Simeon Bar Yochai. We have seen that the Kabbalah teaches that the Holy Serpent is the messiah of the Jews, their God. Albert Pike modeled Freemasonry's 33 rituals and its doctrine based on the teachings of the Kabbalah. According to Pike, the Kabbalah is superior to the Holy Bible. He says that he is "filled with admiration on penetrating into the Sanctuary of the Kabbalah and at seeing a doctrine so simple, yet so absolute."

And who is the author of the Kabbalah? Who is the spiritual genius who gave us this marvelous doctrine "so simple, yet so absolute?" Why, of course, that would be Rabbi Simeon Bar Yochai, the knight in the coffin in the 30th Degree, who presents to us, in Pike's words, the "Mystery of the Kabbalah."

A consensus of Freemasonry's leaders and academics agree totally with Pike. Their guide is the Kabbalah. And the Kabbalah claims that its "God," Ein Sof, has created many "divine sparks," including at least ten gods and goddesses. They are located for our convenience on the Jew's *Tree of Life*. But amidst them all, superintending and directing their divine activities, is none other than the

The House of the Temple in Washington, D.C., where Albert Pike's body is interred. The structure is an exact architectural copy of the tomb of ancient King Mausolus. Our modern word "mausoleum" comes from "Mausolus." The House of the Temple then, is literally a tomb, the house of the dead.

Holy Serpent.

The Holy Serpent, Rabbi Yochai contends in his *Zohar*, which is part of the Kabbalah, is the companion of the Jews. He is their Messiah and represents their God. He is, says the *Zohar*, the equivalent of the Holy Spirit in Christianity.

Rex Hutchens, 33°, author of *A Bridge to Light*, the authoritative textbook published in 1988 by the Supreme Mother Council, the international head of Scottish Rite Freemasonry, affirms this kabbalistic contention. On pages 251-252 of his book, he writes that *"the Universal Agent, the Serpent devouring his own tail"* is, in fact, "the

Inside the sanctuary of the House of the Temple, international headquarters of Scottish Rite Freemasonry, in Washington, D.C. is this black marble altar. Behind, on the wall, are huge serpents. This display is consistent with Rabbi Simeon Bar Yochai's teaching that the Serpent (Satan) is the God to be worshipped by all men.

body of the Holy Spirit."

Christians are shocked and aghast to read Pike, Hutchens, and other top-level Masons acknowledge the Serpent in this way. After all, *Revelation 12:9* clearly refers to "the great dragon... that old serpent, called the Devil and Satan, which deceiveth the whole world."

Serpent the Messiah and Redeemer

Not so, say the rabbis and their spiritual allies in Freemasonry. Famous Rabbi Elijah Ben Solomon, known in Judaism as the Vilna of Gaon, is quoted in Rabbi Yochai's Zohar as teaching that the Serpent is the Messiah and Redeemer of the Jews.

More recently ("Skull & Bones, Freemasonry, and the Serpent Wisdom," online, 2015) Sam LaPoint, 33° Mason, explains the Judaic viewpoint: "The idea that the serpent is evil," says LaPoint, "is a false narrative created by later interpretations of Christianity."

Again, here are those pesky Christians with their "false narrative" which impugns the wonderful Messiah, the Serpent!

According to the Kabbalah and its subordinate Mystery religion, Freemasonry, the Serpent is a most important personage. The Kabbalah teaches that the Serpent *"possesses great illuminating power"* (Rabbi ben Eliezer). The Zohar further teaches that the Serpent is *"the source for universal light."*

Doesn't Albert Pike claim, in *Morals and Dogma*, that Lucifer is the "Light Bearer," the very "Father of Light?" And we who are Christians know that Lucifer, the "Angel of Light," is a synonym for Satan, who is the Serpent.

"In every degree in Freemasonry," says Pike in his book Liturgy, "the candidate seeks to attain Light."

Thus, in every degree in Freemasonry, the candidate draws closer to the Serpent, to Satan, for the Zohar tells us that, *"The Holy Serpent is the fountain head, root, and essence for all God's sacred revelatory light."*

We recall, too, Pike's declaration that Freemasonry is an "ancient Mystery religion." And all the Mystery religions, history reveals, worshipped the Serpent. Rex Hutchens, 33°, on page 100 of *A Bridge to Light*, states, "The priests of the Mysteries were symbolized as a Serpent."

If, indeed, the priests of the Mysteries were symbolized as a Serpent, is it not so that the priests of today's Freemasonry, a Mystery religion according to its founder, Albert Pike, 33°, are also secretly symbolized as Serpents?

Perhaps Pike was, in a sense, correct, when he wrote that the doctrine of the Kabbalah is *"so simple, yet so absolute."*

That doctrine is predicated 100 percent on the imagination of its inventor. And the inventor is the Serpent, the one whom Rabbi Simeon Bar Yochai lionizes and glorifies in the *Zohar* of the Kabbalah.

The upshot: Satan rules Freemasonry under many disguises and ruses, even as the "Light-Bearer."

SIX

About Those "Lost Secrets"

"The Religion of Masonry is not sectarian. It admits men of every creed... It is not Christianity. Its religion is that general one of nature and primitive Revelation—handed down to us from some ancient and patriarchal priesthood..."
>   —Albert Mackey, 33°
>   *Encyclopedia of*
>   *Freemasonry, p. 619*

Here reiterated, is my summation of what is Freemasonry and of whom is worshipped:

"Freemasonry is an ancient Mystery religion involving the worship of Satan and inferior 'deities' through kabbalistic rituals and doctrines taught by the lodges."

Notice again the several elements of Freemasonry:

1. It is an ancient Mystery religion: "It is not Christianity."

2. Members directly or indirectly worship Satan and inferior evil presences through rituals and doctrines taught in the Lodge.

3. These rituals and doctrines originated long ago in the Kabbalah, which is Judaic sorcery.

4. The Masonic Lodge is, in fact, a Synagogue of Satan. (See *Revelation 2* and *3* of the Holy Bible)

As a Mason, are you surprised by this summary? Possibly, it has never been taught or expressed to you in this immediate and direct manner. The Masonic Lodge takes its members piece-meal, step by step into Masonic reality. With each degree and its study, the Mason advances, first toward initiation, then, later, into full demonic possession. By the time the Mason has reached the higher degree levels, say the 27° through the 33°, the individual elements of Freemasonry (ancient Mystery religion, worship of Satan and inferior deities, and Jewish Kabbalism) are often subsumed within one's overall cognitive framework.

George Steinmetz, 33°, in *Freemasonry—It's Hidden Meaning* (Chicago: Charles T. Powner, 1976) stated, "The average Mason is lamentably ignorant of the real meaning of Masonic symbology and knows as little of its esoteric teaching."

Rollin C. Blackmer, another authoritative Mason, in *The Lodge and the Craft* (Richmond, VA: Macoy, 1976) says that, "The great mass of our membership are densely ignorant of everything connected with Masonry."

Freemason, Reverend William H. Russell, in his book, *Masonic Facts for Masons* (Chicago: Charles T. Powner, 1968), remarks that, "Nearly every Mason thinks he knows all about Masonry... As a matter of fact, however, he does not."

If you are a Mason who actually knows little about the Mystery religion you have inadvertently joined, don't feel bad. Most Masons are just like you. You have simply been *"hoodwinked,"* fooled and deceived by Masonic superiors who consider you profane and ignorant.

They see the average Mason as so dumb that he is unworthy of even being told the name of the Masonic God!

They'll first tell you that the name is merely the *Great Architect.* Then, later, they'll confide to you a substitute name, *Mahabone.* Finally, after moving up through the degrees, you discover that the "lost" name is *Jahbulon.* Next, you will learn that you are your own god and you'll be taught to view yourself as an *"Osiris"* (who was, of course, the ancient Sun God of Egypt), and you receive the self-knowledge that *Lucifer* is the Masonic Deity. Yes, that's right—Lucifer! But by that point, it may just be too late for you. You will have gradually and irrevocably been taken in by the ultimate Masonic hoodwink, and be spiritually immobilized forever!

Think, dear friend, do you really want to be spiritually yoked with these unbelievers in the Lodge, who dare not confess the name of Jesus in their corrupt official meetings? Do you really want to be yoked with cultic members of false religions—Islam, Hinduism, Judaism, Buddhism, Jainism, etc.—from around the world, people who deny Jesus Christ and worship other gods? Why is the real name of God kept from the Mason neophyte and "substitutes" given instead?

II Corinthians 6:14-18 provides us the answer why we must stay away from the satanic cult known as Freemasonry:

> *"Be ye not unequally yoked together with unbelievers: for what fellowship hath righteousness with unrighteousness? and what communion hath light with darkness? And what concord hath Christ with Belial? Or what part hath he that believeth with an infidel? And what agreement hath the temple of God with idols? for ye are the temple of the living God; as God hath said, I will dwell in them, and walk in them; and I will be their God, and they shall be my people. Wherefore come out from among them, and be ye separate, saith the Lord, and touch not the unclean thing; and I will receive you, And will be a Father unto you, and ye shall be my sons and daughters, saith the Lord Almighty."*

If you are now a member of the Masonic Lodge, ask yourself, *"Am I unequally yoked with unbelievers?"* How about the Moslem Mason who rejects Jesus Christ as Lord. You have yoked yourself with him, and he is certainly an unbeliever. How about the Jew, whose Talmud claims that Jesus is today "burning in hell in fiery excrement?" And what of the Hindu Mason, who worships the cobra goddess, the rat god, or another of a million so-called Hindu deities?

Masonry Rejects Christianity

If you are a Christian, you worship Christ Jesus. He is God and He alone. Your faith is therefore, according to Freemasonry, *sectarian*, and that is permitted in the lower degrees but is prohibited in the higher degrees of the Masonic Lodge. Listen to what Albert Mackey, author of the *Encyclopedia of Freemasonry* and former Past General High Priest and Secretary General of the Supreme Council, 33rd Degree, stated about the religion of Masonry as contrasted with the *Christian* faith:

> "The religion of Masonry is not sectarian. It admits men of every creed within its hospitable bosom... It is not Christianity... Its religion is that general one of nature and primitive revelation—handed down to us from some ancient and patriarchal priesthood—in which all men may agree and none may differ." (p. 619, *Encyclopedia of Freemasonry*)

This is official Masonic dogma. Other Masons may lie or may skirt around the issue, but above you get it unsugarcoated, from the man who served as "General High Priest" for Freemasons. Mackey is one of today's most respected authorities of Freemasonry, and he flatly says of the religion of Freemasonry:

> *"It is not Christianity."*

What, then, is the religion of Freemasonry? Mackey writes, in his *Encyclopedia of Freemasonry*:

> "If Masonry were simply a Christian institution, the
> Brahmin, the Moslem, and the Buddhist could not
> consciously partake of its illumination, but its
> universality is its boast...at its altars all religions may
> kneel, and to its creed every faith may subscribe."

If you desire a *universalist* religion, a religion based on the dogma of the *Jewish Kabbalah*—which subscribes to numerous gods and goddesses and sorcery of every type—and you do not mind bowing down your knee to a *primitive creed* to which those of any and all religions may subscribe, then *Freemasonry is for you!* But, please, don't claim you are a worshipping Christian.

Remember always: A Christian worships only one God, Jesus Christ, the one who is *not* worshipped at all in the Masonic Lodge. How dare you, therefore, pretend to be a Christian! You, Masonic initiate, are an imposter!

The Masonic God—The Grand Architect

But the Masons do have a Supreme God. We have already reviewed his many names, including Mahabone, Abaddon, and of course, the Grand Architect. Oh yes, he has names and he is above all the Baalim (devils). Albert Pike alludes to Masonry's worship of the "God who is above all the Baalim" when he writes:

> "Masonry around whose altars the Christian, the
> Moslem, the Brahmin, the followers of Confucius and
> Zoroaster, can assemble as brethren and unite in
> prayer to the one God who is above all Baalim..."
> (Pike, *Morals and Dogma*, p. 226).

So, you see, this Masonic Deity does not mind your "silly hagglings" over these many false, sectarian religions like Buddhism, Taoism, Islam, etc. He is above all the Baalim. These other religions are mere halfway houses to the "Father of Light." Eventually, if you stick around long enough you'll discard all the false trappings of inferior religions and fatally embrace the one, true, primitive, universal religion—Freemasonry.

SEVEN

Freemasonry is an Ancient Mystery Religion Based on the Judaic Kabbalah

"The old primitive faith that is the Freemasonry religion is derived from the Ancient pure Kabbalah."
—Albert Pike, 33°
Morals and Dogma

Freemasonry, say its advocates, is not simply a religion. Freemasonry is *the* religion. It is the primitive religion, which was first taught man.

Albert Pike, in *Morals and Dogma*, writes, "Masonry teaches, and has preserved in their purity, the cardinal tenets of the old primitive faith."

What exactly is this "old primitive faith" that today is called "Freemasonry?" It is not Christianity, for Pike and most all the Masonic experts insist that Freemasonry

95

predates Christianity and has its own creed.

> "Masonry propagates no creed except its own most simple and Sublime One; that universal religion, taught by nature and reason." (Pike, *Morals And Dogma*)

So Christians—and Moslems, Buddhists, Hindus, etc.—must understand that Freemasonry is not based on any modern-day creed such as Christianity or Islam, but is instead the "old primitive faith" that is universal.

Freemasonry Derived From the "Ancient Pure Kabbalah"

Pike goes on to say that the "old primitive faith" that is the Freemasonry religion is derived from the *"Ancient pure Kabbalah."* The Kabbalah, of course, is one of the prime contributors to the religion we know as Judaism. Therefore, the roots of Freemasonry are kabbalistic and include, adds Pike, the belief in the ineffable, non-communicative god. This god is called Ein Sof in the Kabbalah and its ten subordinates are deities, called emanations, or sparks, of light which proceed from this universal Deity known as Ein Sof (Pike, *Morals and Dogma*, p. 727).

Rex Hutchens, in his book, *A Bridge to Light*, published in 1988 by the Supreme Mother council, 33° in Washington, D.C., explains:

> "Pike believed that certain ancient cultures possessed the Truth that God had originally given to man...a more accurate and comprehensive knowledge of the

Deity and his relationship to the universe and man
than modern philosophies and religions."

As we can see, Christianity, a "modern religion" according to Masons, is inadequate. Long before the advent of this Christian faith, "God had originally given to man...a more accurate and comprehensive knowledge..."

How splendid that God had already given man *a more accurate and comprehensive knowledge.*" But then, why was Jesus' New Covenant necessary to complete the old Covenant of the Jews if this were so? Since, as Pike told us, the *"Ancient pure Kabbalah"* is the instrument that God had first devised to bring to man this "more accurate and comprehensive knowledge," one wonders whether Jesus at his advent was not aware of its more perfect "teachings?"

Rex Hutchens, the Masonic author of *A Bridge to Light*, goes on to explain that man therefore must know of the Kabbalah and its Sephiroth (inferior deities) to understand truth:

"Albert Mackey (former Sovereign Grand Commander
of Scottish Rite Freemasonry) in his Masonic
Encyclopedia noted that ...some acquaintance with
the Kabbalah, therefore, seems to be necessary to the
Freemason." (*A Bridge to Light*, p. 250)

The Kabbalah is far better in its instruction than what Jesus or His apostles taught in the New Testament because, Hutchens assures us, it teaches complete truth:

"The ancient and accepted rite fulfills the function of both King and Priest for its duty is to teach truth in all its varied aspects—moral, political, philosophical and religious." (*A Bridge to Light*, p. 260)

So we now have Pike, Mackey, and Hutchens all agreed on the superiority of the Kabbalah religion of Freemasonry to the religion of Jesus Christ. Virtually, every Masonic authority agrees that the Kabbalah is at the foundation of everything Masonic. It is Truth. The Masonic Lodge holds the Kabbalah in the highest esteem.

As *Coil's Masonic Encyclopedia* remarks, the "basic doctrine and tradition of the Masonic Lodge is Judaic." (*Coil's Masonic Encyclopedia*, p. 512)

So Freemasonry claims to be a religion, the first and foremost of all religions. It is based on the occultic Jewish Kabbalah and cannot be separated from these theological roots. Delmar Darrah, 33°, in his textbook, *History and Evolution of Freemasonry* (Charles Powner, 1979) emphasizes, in fact, that, "the religious element...is its most distinguishing characteristic," and that if there 'were no Kabbalah, there would be no Freemasonry." Darrah says further that, "Masonry discards as nonessential...the old religious ideas."

According to Darrah, Freemasonry religion "is simply the result of a long, tedious process of evolution during which man has advanced from a mere brute to the highest product of modern civilization."

There you have it. Freemasonry, a Kabbalah Mystery religion, was produced by the *evolutionary process* of succeeding emanations. Whereas, Christianity is a *revelatory* religion. Christianity was revealed to man by God, but Masonry claims that man himself discovered through evolution the superiority of the Masonic religion.

The founder of Christianity is, of course, Jesus Christ. But Freemasonry has the Kabbalah and its disciples as its co-founders and these men favor no other religion. They have their own; the Lodge and its "primitive faith."

> "These early founders of Masonry conceived a system of moral religion at whose shrine all men might worship, the Christian, the Catholic, the Protestant, the Confucian, the Buddhist, the Mohammedan, as well as all others who are willing to acknowledge a supreme being and live a life of moral rectitude." (Darrah, *History And Evolution of Freemasonry*, p. 290-300)

Christianity is an Inferior Sectarian Religion

If you are a Christian, or profess Christianity, you are a sectarian. The Masons will be glad to have you *also* join their occult fraternity and take part in *their* religion, which is, they insist, more complete, has more "truth," and is the only "universal" religion. The same goes for the Buddhist, the Moslem and members of all other world religions. Their members are welcome to become Masons, but will be taught that their *sectarian* faith is inferior to the Masonic faith which is based on the superior Judaic Kabbalah.

This bargain with the Devil, the willing embrace of a supposedly superior religion based on the Kabbalah, seems to be acceptable to the millions of Masons now active in the Masonic Lodge. The syncretic *mixture* of pagan religion (Freemasonry) and Christianity is even celebrated by some Masons.

Going to a Lodge meeting can be like attending an *interfaith* worship service, they say. At the Lodge, you can associate with people of all religions. You can practice your great tolerance and respect for Islam, Hinduism, Zoroastrianism, and especially Judaism. This hodge-podge of religious faiths must, however, all give allegiance to the superior, primitive *religion* that binds them all as One.

They must not and cannot say that their *sectarian* faith is better than any other man's sectarian faith. That would be an "anti-Mason" attitude and demonstrate horrific non-acceptance of the "universal truth" found only in the Mystery teachings of the Lodge.

We see, then, that Freemasonry is derived from the "ancient, pure, primitive" faith found in the Judaic Kabbalah. But this faith has over time been improved upon as men evolved spiritually. The ancient religions of Egypt, Babylon, Greece, Rome and others were used to formulate Freemasonry, but the knowledge of Kabbalah is the *capstone*:

> "With the unveiling of great spiritual truths by the Hebrew writers, and the reflection of Divine light upon the mysteries of many ancient religions through these revelations, Masonry became the depository of the Divine Truth in its symbols, traditions, legends, and mysteries and has preserved Truth through all the centuries of the past."

Masonry only is the "depository of Divine Truth," we are told. It is based, the writer tells us, on symbols, traditions, legends, and mysteries. We recall Jesus warning that the Jews had for their religion, not instruction from the Divine, but had the "traditions of elders," the "traditions of men." Their heads and eyes were therefore fixed not on God's laws, but on Satan and his devices (see *Matthew 23*)

Christianity is Overlaid with Error

Pike explains this as follows. He twists this truth when he writes that all of man's other sectarian religions are based solely on "the works of men."

> "All that ever existed have had a basis of truth; and all have overlaid that truth with error." (*Morals and Dogma*, p. 161)

Christianity, then, is merely the "work of men" and has some truth but also a lot of error. It comes, says Pike, from a particular world region or country, and is "adopted to the usages, manners, and prejudices of particular countries" (*Morals and Dogma*, p. 161).

Christianity, Pike claims, is inferior to the primitive and universal religion taught and practiced in Masonry because of its narrow, regional focus. But the Masonic faith, set upon the pillars of the Judaic Kabbalah, is, he writes, "the universal morality which is suitable to the inhabitants of every clime, to the man of every creed." (*Morals and Dogma*, p. 161)

It is thus necessary, adds Pike, acknowledged as the

"Master Builder" of Freemasonry and Father of its 33 degree rituals, for men to push on past the "mythologies" of their childhood religion.

"The progressive man," says Pike, "goes ever forth to fresh fields and pastures new." *(Morals and Dogma*, pp. 161-162)

In attaining higher Masonic degrees and especially the 27th and 30th degrees of Freemasonry, the candidate takes an oath to follow and obey these better teachings. He says he will, indeed, abandon the myths taught him as a child by his sectarian religion (Christianity, Islam, etc.) and go forward toward his supposed high calling as a Mason.

See what you have to look forward to as a lower-level Mason? You will eventually be challenged by the Lodge to ditch the Christian principles and foundation you were taught by your parents and by your Church. Make up your mind now what you will do. *The wrong decision will surely weigh on you for all eternity.*

EIGHT

Is the Masonic Lodge "Mystery Babylon?"

"Beware lest any man spoil you through philosophy and vain deceit, after the traditions of men, after the rudiments of the world, and not after Christ."
—Colossians 2:8

According to Pike, Hall, Wilmshurst, and all the "great" scholars and leaders of Freemasonry, the Masonic Lodge comes straight out of Babylon. Anyone who denies this fact is simply an idiot who knows nothing of Freemasonry.

Now I am sure you expect me to prove this Babylonian connection, and I will. It is my pleasure to do so. But first, let's examine what the Holy Bible has to say about *"Mystery, Babylon the Great."*

Mystery Babylon is mentioned extensively in the Bible. Babylon is one of the great cities of the ancients. It was founded by the wicked King, Nimrod, and his seductive and alluring wife, Queen Semiramis. After Nimrod's death, Semiramis incestuously married their son, Tammuz, claiming that Tammuz was the reincarnation of his father, Nimrod. Thus, the pagan trinity of Father, Mother, and Son came into being. Today, Freemasonry continues its adoration and worship of the pagan trinity, including the Hindu version in its higher degrees.

Now it was at Babylon, in Sumaria (today Babylon is in Iraq) where the infamous Tower of Babel was built. We read in *Genesis 11:1-4*:

> *"And the whole earth was of one language, and of one speech. And it came to pass, as they journeyed from the east, that they found a plain in the land of Shinar, and they dwelt there...And they said, go to, let us build a city and tower, whose top may reach unto heaven."*

Here we see the *hubris*, or pride of the Babylonians. They wanted to extend their city into heaven. They wanted to become higher "gods." They were united in this vain effort. But of course, the Bible records that God confounded them, by making the people speak different languages. Confused and disunited, the Tower building project fell into disarray and ruin.

Demon Powers Guide Freemasons

The Masons of today continue in their vainglorious quest for supremacy. They now attempt to unite all religions and cults in a fantastic spiritual building project, and they are assisted in these efforts by demons who are the invisible powers behind Freemasonry and its deceptive, secretive Mystery Religion.

Listen to what Manly P. Hall, 33°, says on page 58 of his book, *What the Ancient Wisdom Expects of Its Disciples*:

> "The ancient initiates are the invisible powers behind the thrones of earth, and men are but marionettes, dancing while the invisible ones pull the strings. We see the dancer, but the master mind that does the work remains concealed by the cloak of silence."

Who are these "ancient initiates" to whom Hall refers? The Mason will meet them in the higher degrees. Albert Pike, in *Morals and Dogma* explains that in the 32nd Degree, "The true initiate is both King and Priest over the people."

So listen up, Mason, you have an invisible initiate watching over you, directing your path. You are not independent as you so smugly pretend. The initiates are both "King and Priest" over you!

"Mystery Babylon, Mother of Harlots and Abominations of the Earth"

In *Revelation 13*, the scriptures tell us that Mystery Babylon is a whorish religion that spreads throughout the world in the last days. She's a monstrous killer of truth and a dealer in death to men and women. In *Revelation 17*, Mystery Babylon rides the Beast of prophecy.

Could Freemasonry be the horrific "Mother of Harlots?" Is Freemasonry, like the Woman, drunken with the blood of the saints and the martyrs of Jesus? What do the masses themselves say about their ancient connection with Mystery Babylon?

Mystery Babylon is the "Mother" of all the Mystery religions, and these Mystery religions spread throughout the world after the confounding of the Builders at the Tower of Babel. Mystery religions prevailed in ancient Greece, Rome, Egypt, Sumaria, Persia, China, Tibet, North Africa and the Americas. (In the Americas, the Incas, the Mayans, the Toltecs, and others are examples). But it was in Babylon that the Mystery Religion first flourished and became illustrious and decadent.

In his Masonic textbook, *Morals and Dogma*, Albert Pike waxes rhapsodic about all these "great" Mystery religions. He describes them, one after another, and he notes their positive identity with Freemasonry, which, he and other Masons contend, is the Mystery Religion *par excellence*. They are all religions, but Freemasonry, claims Pike, is *the* religion.

According to Pike, Freemasonry existed "from the cradle of the human race:"

> "But, by whatever name it was known in this or the other country, Masonry existed as it now exists, the same in spirit and heart...before even the first colonies emigrated into Southern India, Persia, and Egypt, from the cradle of the human race." (pp. 207-208)

Quite an admission, isn't it? And Pike goes on to say that in almost all these ancient Mystery religions, of which Freemasonry is most prominent, the worshippers adored the *Holy Serpent*, by whatever name he was called.

Builders of the Tower of Babel Were Masons

Now, if Freemasonry is really this ancient, then its founders, whether real or legendary, were also ancient. And if Freemasonry was the first and the most pre-eminent of Mystery Religions, and if it can be traced back to the very *"cradle of the human race,"* then it had its origins in the Garden of Eden, where Lucifer seduced

A painting of the famous, unfinished Tower of Babel in Babylon. Freemasonry claims that Nimrod, King of ancient Babylon, was an esteemed member of the Masonic fraternity. Also, the Masons say that Peleg, architect of the Tower, was also a Mason.

Eve first, and Adam and Eve suffered the Great Fall.

From the expulsion time of Adam and Eve from the Garden of Eden, we find cities being built, first by Cain and then by others. Finally, in Mesopotamia, the city of Babylon was built with its infamous Tower of Babel. There, as we discussed, Nimrod was King.

Could *Nimrod* have been a Freemason? That is exactly what we are told in the *Encyclopedia of Freemasonry*! The *Encyclopedia*, in fact, says that Nimrod was one of the founders of Masonry.

Nimrod, the wicked self-proclaimed "God" and Nimrod, the *"Hunter of Men"* (see the book of *Genesis* in the Holy Bible), a founder of Freemasonry? That is exactly what the Masonic Lodge claims. And so we have this incredible connection between ancient Babylon and Modern Freemasonry.

The *"Oath of Nimrod"* is a feature of the initiation process for the Indentured Apprentice Degree (see Spring 2006 issue of *Freemasonry Today*).

In his scholarly book, *The Arcana of Freemasonry*, Albert Churchward includes the text of the "Oath of Nimrod." The penalty for the Freemason revealing this oath is nothing less than the forfeiture of his life.

Christian researcher, Cathy Burns in her excellent *Masonic and Occult Symbols Illustrated* gives two examples of the Masonic Lodge's connection to the heaven-accursed Tower of Babel. In the *Masonic Quiz Book* the authors say that Nimrod, king of Babylon responsible for the Tower fiasco, is referred to in Masonry as "One of the founders of Masonry, and in the Scriptures as the architect of many cities."

Meanwhile, in a document called the York manuscript we find this glowing account of the Tower of Babel:

> "At the making of the Tower of Babel there was Masonry much esteemed...Nimrod was a Mason himself and loved well Masons."

Nimrod, history records, was a very wicked ruler who sponsored abominable sorcery and magical practices His Mystery religion in Babylon offered human sacrifices, practiced incest and sexual witchcraft, introduced astrology and divination, worshipped various demonic entities, and exercised fire and sun worship.

And the Masons of today boast that their founder, Nimrod "was a Mason himself who loved well Masons."

Tower of Babel a Masonic Enterprise

Evidence is abundant that the Masons are extremely proud of their ancient Tower of Babel, built by beings disrespectful and disobedient to God in heaven. Arthur Edward Waite, editor of *A New Encyclopedia of Freemasonry*, reveals that, "The Candidate (for the Noachite or Prussian Knight Degree) is shown the Tower of Babel and the Mausoleum of Peleg," its Grand Architect.

Waite also states, "As regards Masonry, Babel, of course, represented a Masonic enterprise."

John Yarker, another highly esteemed scholar and author, writes, "It is well-known that the Tower of Babel was one of the ancient traditions of Masonry."

Now, whether the Tower of Babel narrative is simply

a fictitious tale by Masons proud of its structure or is true history is irrelevant. The fact is, Masonry wants the world to know that the Masons are responsible for this incredible affront to Almighty God. It is their project—and the Devil's.

Peleg, the Architect of the Tower of Babel, is Honored

Nimrod is not the only member of the ancient Babylonian people and builder of the Tower who is recognized by today's Freemasons. The architect of the Tower of Babel is also honored by the Masonic Lodge in the 21st degree, that of Noachite, or the Prussian Knight Degree:

> "This Degree stands alone in Masonry... In this Degree a man named Peleg is the Founder of this Degree by virtue of his position as the Grand Architect of the Tower of Babel. He is said to have traveled to Prussia during the dispersion where he died. In AD 553 his tombstone was found with the inscription: "Here rests the ashes of Peleg, our Grand Architect of the Tower of Babel."

According to the Masons, Peleg, Grand Architect of the Tower of Babel, a structure erected by prideful would-be man-gods and destroyed by God from heaven, *"is blessed by Almighty God because he is such a humble man."* Say What?! Are you kidding me?

Masonry is Identical to the Ancient Mysteries

Albert Pike brags in *Morals and Dogma*:

"Masonry is identical to the ancient mysteries." (p. 624)

Think about this eye-opening admission: *"Masonry is identical to the ancient Mysteries."*

Now, go to any of hundreds of scholarly books and encyclopedias on the topic of the ancient Mystery religions. Read about their worship of serpents, their temple prostitution, their divination, necromancy (communication with spirits), their astrology, their witchcraft, and of their many other abominations. Then, read again Pike's statement: *"Masonry is identical to the ancient Mysteries."*

It is a certainty that the Mysteries are the work of Satan. Thus, Freemasonry is the work of Satan for, as Pike boldly stated, *"Masonry is identical to the ancient Mysteries."*

Scholar G.H. Pember, in *Earth's Earliest Ages*, writes:

> "There is little doubt that the culmination of the Mysteries was the worship of Satan himself."

George Otterman, in his informative article, "Hermeneutics 101: Forbidden Knowledge and Mystery Religions," stated:

> "Mystery religions worship a deity, and without exception, it is the Devil..."

Helena Blavatsky, a woman co-Mason and Theosophist, in *The Secret Doctrine* reveals that it is *Lucifer*, the one whom Christians know as Satan or the Devil who is worshipped in the Mysteries as God.

David Wood, author of *Genesis: The First Book of Revelation*, says that in the Mysteries, the worshippers find that Satan is God: "In all that was Holy was Satan."

"We have seriously misjudged Satan," writes Wood, "He is Rex Mundi, King of the World."

David Wood is an avid proponent of the Jewish Kabbalah, the same Mystery teaching subscribed to by Albert Pike and the Masonic Order. It is from the Mysteries of the Kabbalah that Pike fashioned his 33-degree rituals.

The Kabbalah despises and hates Christianity and it blasphemes our Lord and Saviour, Jesus Christ. It was written, say the Jews, by, one Rabbi Simeon Bar Yochai, who is honored by Freemasonry in its 30-degree ritual. Rabbi Bar Yochai hated the Christian faith. His Judaic Law, *"The best of the Christians—kill!"* is found recorded in the Babylonian Talmud, the rulebook for today's Judaism.

Knowing how demonic and blasphemous the Talmud and Kabbalah are we turn again to the religion of Freemasonry which is, according to Pike, *"identical with the Mysteries,"* we can only agree with G.H. Pember, who advises, "There is little doubt that the culmination of the Mysteries was the worship of Satan himself."

Pike revealed himself and Freemasonry for what they truly are when he wrote in *Morals and Dogma* of the perverse kabbalistic belief that Satan is a "most occult light." Christians know that, instead, Satan often comes *disguised* as an angel of light, but Pike wrote:

> "The true name of Satan, the Kabbalists say, is
> Yahweh (God) reversed; for Satan is not a negation of
> God... The Kabbalah imagined him to be 'a most
> occult light.'"

NINE

Freemasonry is Not Christianity and Has Little To Do With the Holy Bible

"There is yet another misconception about Judaism which is particularly common among Christians...This is the misleading idea that Judaism is a 'biblical religion'; that the Old Testament in Judaism has the same central place and legal authority which the Bible has for Protestant or even Catholic Christianity..."

—Israel Shahak
Jewish History, Jewish Religion

The doctrines, or dogma, of Freemasonry are outlined in great detail by Masonic scholars such as Manly P. Hall, 33°, Albert Pike, 33°, Albert Mackey, 33°, and W. L. Wilmshurst,

33°. These scholars uniformly tell us in their writings—
and it is stated clearly in the thirty-three rituals of
Freemasonry—that the dogma of the Lodge comes from
the Jewish Kabbalah.

In *Morals and Dogma*, the quintessential doctrinal
guide to Freemasonry by Albert Pike, former Grand
Commander, Supreme Council of 33rd Degree Scottish
Rite Freemasonry, we read:

> "All truly dogmatic religions have issued from the
> Kabbalah and return to it; everything scientific and
> grand in the religious dreams of all the Illuminati...is
> borrowed from the Kabbalah; all Masonic associations
> owe to it their Secrets and their Symbols." (p. 744)

What a statement of belief. Pike, recognized as the
"Father of Modern Freemasonry," tells us that, "All truly
dogmatic religions have issued from the Kabbalah and
return to it." Masonry is a dogmatic religion, owing to
the Kabbalah its "Secrets" and "Symbols."

Therefore, for a student of Freemasonry to know all
of Freemasonry's secrets and symbols, that student must
turn to the Kabbalah. It is the vast reservoir and depository
of Freemasonry dogma.

But, asks the Christian, what of the Holy Bible, that
great book which he has long been told is the foundation
stone of his faith and his daily guide for living?

The Holy Bible, set to an Old Testament verse, sits on
the altar in the Lodge, but it is disregarded and not used.
The Kabbalah has little use for the Scriptures, and in
other countries a Lodge may place the Hindu Veda, the

Islamic Koran, or perhaps Albert Pike's book, *Morals and Dogma*, on the altar.

Professor Israel Shahak of Hebrew University in Israel explains why. He writes:

> "There is yet another misconception about Judaism which is particularly common among Christians...This is the misleading idea that Judaism is a 'biblical religion'; that the Old Testament in Judaism has the same central place and legal authority which the Bible has for Protestant or even Catholic Christianity..." (*Jewish History, Jewish Religion*, by Israel Shahak, Pluto Press, 1994)

Reginald Haupt, in his authoritative guide, *The Gods of the Lodge*, confirms this. He writes, "Masonry has nothing to do with the Bible. No special authority is placed on the Old or New Testament. A Masonic Lodge of Muslims substitute the Koran, a predominantly Hindu Lodge the Vedas, etc." *The Digest of Masonic Law*, written by George Wingate Chase, makes it abundantly clear at page 207:

> "To say that a candidate profess a belief in the divine authority of the Bible is a serious innovation in the very body of Masonry. The Jews, the Chinese, the Turks, each reject either the Old or the New Testament, or both, and yet we see no good reason why they should not be made Masons. In fact, Blue Lodge Masonry (first 3 degrees) has nothing whatever to do with the Bible; it is not founded on the Bible. If it

was, it would not be Masonry. It would be something else."

Take note of Chase's last three sentences. Masonry *"is not founded on the Bible. If it was, it would not be Masonry. It would be something else."*

Masonry Based on the Kabbalah

Pike also explains that, "everything scientific and grand is borrowed from the Kabbalah." Therefore, to grasp the work and dogma of all the Illuminati; we once again turn to the Kabbalah.

It is fortuitous that this is so because I have spent much of my life examining and studying the Jewish Kabbalah and the Jewish philosophers who promote and publish the doctrines found therein. I have recently written five books devoted to the Kabbalah, including *Conspiracy of the Six-Pointed Star, The Destroyer, Holy Serpent of the Jews, Feast of the Beast*, and *Hell's Mirror*. In addition, my earlier books, *New Age Cults and Religions, Dark Secrets of the New Age, Mystery Mark of the New Age*, and *Ravaged by the New Age* meticulously examine the many cults and false religions spawned by the Kabbalah.

I am also author of *Mysterious Monuments*, an encyclopedic book in which I review and critique the corrupt architecture and teachings of the Mystery religions of antiquity and the modern era. Another book which has had a great impact is my *Codex Magica*, an illustrated handbook to the secret symbols, hand signs, and coded language of the Masonic Lodge and of various illuminist secret societies and Mystery religions.

As demonstrated in my many books, Judaism is a tragically misunderstood religion. Christians mistakenly believe that the Jews practice Old Testament religion.

In fact, Jewish rabbis know little of the books of the Old Testament. They attend years in a Yeshiva (religious seminary) but many spend not a day studying the Old Testament, which their instructors tell them is full of myths and legends and is not worthy of their time. However, depending on the Yeshiva and its emphasis, much time is spent on both the Babylonian Talmud and the Kabbalah. Increasingly, the Kabbalah is the preferred tool of Judaic study.

The Talmud and Kabbalah are both vital to Judaic teachings, and the Talmud includes much commentary and instruction from the Kabbalah. While both are products of men, the Kabbalah is claimed to have been inspired by angels.

Kabbalah Is at the Very Heart of Judaism

The Kabbalah is at the very heart of Judaism. It grips the Jew with its bizarre doctrinal structure and introduces a fascinating array of mystical, magical practices. These magical practices include the use of secret symbols, gematria (the magic of numerology), astrology, angelology, necromancy (communication with the dead), chanting, mantras, goddess worship and sexual magic, divination, color mysticism, alteration of consciousness, psychic mind powers, idol worship, and many other elements of witchcraft and black magic.

The Kabbalah is a Mystery religion, traceable back to Babylon, Egypt, Greece, Rome, Asia Minor and North

Africa. A study of the many Mystery religions is enlightening. The Jew is persuaded by his racist rabbi superior that the Kabbalah is exclusive to the Jews but, in fact, it is based on universalist dogma. That is why Freemasonry has adopted the Kabbalah as its foundation for doctrine, morals, and as a guide for all its degrees. Masons are thereby able to claim universal Mystery religion status while simultaneously portraying their religion as Judaic.

Some Christians enthusiastically join the Lodge because they are practicing a loose form of Judaism. The symbols are often the same as employed in synagogues; religious language and history which sound like that in the Old Testament is heard and even the names of the 33 degrees often have Jewish titles. Most Christian denominations—Southern Baptist, Methodist, Episcopal, etc.—are extremely Judeo-centric. Many churches romanticize the Jewish festivals and greatly exalt Judaic heroes from the Holy Bible. Under the circumstances, the Christian feels "at home" in the Lodge with its kabbalistic Judaism moorings and environment.

The Christian overlooks or diminishes in his mind the Lodge's constant complementary emphasis on the many historic Mystery religions. He believes the study of these antiquated Mystery religions is merely for his further education and enlargement of his knowledge.

Masonry Opposed to Sectarianism

The Masonic authorities ingeniously and repeatedly use the drumbeat of Mystery religion propaganda to divert their members away from sectarianism, which is the avowed principal enemy of the Masonic Lodge. Sectarianism, that is, elevation and worship by the individual of his specific monotheistic religion—in this case, Christianity, is *forbidden*. The exaltation of the name of Jesus as Lord and Saviour is not allowed in the Masonic rituals. That is sectarianism, and since Masonry is based on the universalistic Mystery religion of Kabbalism, Sectarianism is strictly prohibited.

Sectarian religions such as Christianity, Islam, and Buddhism are assigned by Freemasonry to the status of just another limited religious system. The Holy Bible, the Koran, and other holy books are considered as "furniture" in the Lodge and there are no body of teachings of Jesus, Buddha, Mohammed, engaged in by the Lodge.

The insistence by a lower-level Christian Mason of his continued exclusive worship of Jesus Christ will blunt his climb up the degree ranks and he will be judged as unfitting for high Masonic office. Subordination of his sectarian faith is the desired route for Masons.

The Mason will discover by the 30th degree that to receive more "light" as a Mason, he is expected to *abandon* his exclusive belief in Jesus as Lord and Saviour. He must then renounce Jesus and embrace Masonry only. At that point, the Mason may keep his useless title of "Christian" Baptist, Episcopal, etc., but he knows this title is only for social purposes, or to please family or community, or for tradition.

Masonry the Only True Religion?

In the 30th degree, toleration by the Mason of Christianity and other religions will end. He will affirm that Masonry is the only true religion and that exclusive belief in inferior gods like Jesus is unacceptable. It will not be tolerated.

However, Masonry's highest authorities and top scholars agree, without argument, that Freemasonry is ultimately the same religion as Judaism. And that is why Jews pack the Masonic Lodges. They find in its rituals, dogma, and mysticism a worthy version of their very own religion. Freemasonry is Judaism.

If Masonry downgrades Jesus Christ, dismisses the Holy Bible and insists that it is something other than Christianity, why do some Masons doggedly hold on to their identification as "Christians?"

Could it be that, in fact, they are *not* Christians but are pseudo-Christians, imitation believers possessing a lukewarm faith? Did Jesus not say that, "many are called but few are *chosen?" (Matthew 20:16)*. Did he not also warn that those who are neither cold nor hot but are lukewarm, he will spew them out of his mouth" *(Revelation 3:15-16)*?

Lucifer, the Light Bearer, Invites You to His House of Light

"The criers of the Mysteries speak again, bidding all men welcome to the House of Light."
—Manly P. Hall, 33°
The Secret Teaching of All Ages

W e see, then, that Masonry, by the admission of the official spokesmen of the Masonic Lodge—its 33° representative, Sovereign Grand Commanders—is a Judaic religion. As such, its adherents testify that their allegiance is not to the doctrine of the Holy Bible, but to those in the Kabbalah.

Albert Mackey, in *The Encyclopedia of Freemasonry* (Volume 1, p. 166) repeats that all of the secrets and symbols of Freemasonry originate in the books of the Kabbalah, which is said to come from the Jews:

> "The mystical philosophy or theosophy of the Jews is called the Kabbalah. The Word is derived from the Hebrew Kabal, signifying to receive, because it is the doctrine received from the elders."

According to Masonry, kabbalism is a very old and primitive, universalist Mystery religion. From the Kabbalah came all the world's many Mystery religions. Only it has the answers that reveal where man comes from and where he is going. In his *Revised Encyclopedia of Freemasonry*, (Volume 1, p. 166), Albert Mackey, 33°, one of Masonry's greatest scholars, states:

> "The Kabbalah was first taught by God to a select company of angels, who formed a theosophic school in paradise. After the fall, the angels most graciously communicated this heavenly doctrine to the disobedient child of earth..."

Do you grasp what Mackey is telling readers here? He is claiming that the Kabbalah originated first in heaven (Paradise), being learned and taught by a "select company of angels."

After the fall, according to the Masonic encyclopedia, the angels taught this "heavenly doctrine" (the Kabbalah) to the "disobedient child of earth." These legions of Lucifer continued their wicked rebellion on earth, communicating these bizarre and error-filled visions to "the disobedient child on earth." That would be Adam.

Mackey's encyclopedia claims further that the secrets of Kabbalah were communicated from Adam to Noah.

Now since the teachings of Kabbalah include unholy knowledge of the forbidden tree of knowledge of good and evil and also communicate lies and misinformation about God and the Elohim, we begin to understand the magnitude of deception wrapped up in the doctrines of Kabbalah.

There can be no doubt that the Kabbalah is the most vile religion ever constructed and thus we understand why the Masons have bought into its multitude of lies. The Masonic Lodge reveals in this case that the Kabbalah is a masterpiece of deception supposedly composed first by rebellious angels who, after the fall, communicated its foul doctrines to mankind, first to Adam, and then on to Noah, Moses, David, and Solomon, and later to millions of Jews and other human beings by use of the fictitious myths and legends of a multitude of Mystery religions which spread across the planet earth.

Today, the Kabbalah continues to spread its poisonous teachings through Judaism and Masonry, as well as a vast number of New Age cults and religions. The millions of men and women who today grow intoxicated and cold to the Truth are gripped by devils and rendered immobile to the Gospel. They are truly the *"sons of disobedience"* and they now await the Great White Throne judgement.

Masons Teach Tolerance and "Accept" All Religions

The Devil has thus made the Kabbalah his chief instrument of human recruitment. It is easy to understand why the Kabbalah serves in such an universalist capacity. First, and most important is the working of the God of the Kabbalah. We know him as Satan, or Lucifer, but his identity is at first rendered unclear to the Jew and to the Mason...In the Masonic Lodge, the name of Deity is made mysterious and the Mason works through numerous degrees attempting to discover his true identity. It is the *Lost Word* he seeks.

Masons are told that their Deity holds the title of *Grand Architect of the Universe (GAOTU)*. The "G" letter prominently displayed in lodges on the wall behind the altar is said to mean *"God"* or stands for Grand Geometrician or Geometry but this is not the Lost Word. Later, he is told that there is a substitute name he can use in referring to the Deity. That would be Mahabone. In the 13th degree, the Mason actually declares himself God. When asked, "who are you?," he blasphemously replies, "I am that I am."

Still later, it is revealed to him that the "sacred word" is *Abaddon*. But the naïve Mason learns this is yet another title of the God and so he must continue to strive to discover the Lost Word, the real name. He is told he needs *"more light."*

Now, at this point in his Masonic career, when he is told in the 17th degree that the Sacred Word is *Abaddon*, which, in Hebrew means "Destroyer," this should be a clue that the religion of Masonry is a dangerous and wicked religion. If he were a Bible student, the Masonic initiate might have read *Revelation 9* where we read of a star falling from heaven unto earth: *"And to him was given the key of the bottomless pit."*

From the pit of hell rise demonic creatures like locusts, *"and they had tails like scorpions and there were stings in their tails and their power was to hurt men five months."*

> *"And they had a king over them, which is the angel of the bottomless pit, whose name in the Hebrew tongue is Abaddon." (Revelation 9:11)*

Masons Exhibit "666" Sign and Are Told That "Jahbulon" is "God"

It is in the Royal Arch degree, York Rite, that the Masonic initiate learns yet another name for the Deity whom he worships as Grand Architect of the Universe. In the ritual, a "666" symbol is executed by three Masons and the "ineffable name" is made known to the candidate: *"Jah-Bul-On."* Jahbulon is a composite name for the Masonic Deity but is not the final, lasting name. It stands for a combination of three specific gods—*Jahweh (Jah)*, the God of the Hebrews, *Baal*, or *Bul*, the ancient, Canaanite fertility god that led the Jews into licentious sex rites of magic and lust, and finally, *On*, a name which stands for the Egyptian Lord of the Dead, the Sun god *Osiris*.

So Jahbulon is the Masonic worship of "God" as three combined deities, Jahweh, Baal, and On. How much more blatantly blasphemous can you get? The Masons literally mock the true God and call him by horrible, sinful names that typify devilish lust and black magic.

At this stage, having progressed from Mahabone to Abaddon and now Jahbulon, there can be no doubt Masonry is the worship of none other than *Lucifer* and the names used for him in the Masonic rituals are reserved for devils. Even the name Jahweh denotes not the Jehovah, the Great I Am of the Old Testament, but instead is the title of a tribal Lord worshipped by the ancient, primitive Jewish people.

Even after this recognition of great evil by the Mason, the Lost Word is hidden from him. But the initiate cannot escape the fact that he worships *Lucifer, the Devil*, who is symbolized in the book of *Revelation* as the *Serpent*. With every degree ritual he draws closer to this monstrous conclusion.

The Candidate Seeks "More Light"

"In every degree in Freemasonry," says Pike in his book, *Liturgy*, "the candidate seeks to attain Light. It is for each individual Mason to discover the secret of Masonry...seek and ye shall find."

The candidate is constantly encouraged to study Masonic books and Masonic Law to supplement and augment the knowledge he has attained directly in the Lodge. Albert Pike's classic text, *Morals and Dogma* is a chief resource, and in studying Pike, the meaning of the Lost Word rises over and over in his mind. Pike reveals there are in Kabbalism two main deities, and one of them is Lucifer. Lucifer, the Father of Light, he who rewarded Adam and Eve for their disobedience in the Garden. Did he not also give the "son of disobedience" (see *Ephesians 2:1,2*) the secrets of the Kabbalah?

So what does Pike say to the Mason who constantly seeks more Light about Lucifer, the one whom Manly P. Hall, 33° later says is the Master of the "House of Light?"

First, a soothing Pike assures the Mason that, "There is no rebellious demon of Evil or Principle of Darkness in eternal controversy with God."

Next, he embraces the kabbalistic doctrine that Lucifer is companion of man, a good angel:

> "For the Initiates this is not a person but a force, created for good, but which may serve for evil. It is the instrument of Liberty or Free Will."

In the book of *Daniel*, God testifies that the last days antichrist will be the "God of Forces." Pike writes that Lucifer is a "force." As for "Liberty" and "Free Will," these are codewords of Satan, and his human agents insist they wish to bring men "Liberty" from tyrannical religion, and "Free Will," meaning the use of Reason without compulsion by God. The Satanist does not honor the will of God...Pike states:

> "Human reason leaps into the throne of God and waves her torch over the ruins of the universe."

Pike is adamant about dethroning the true God and giving the reason of man sovereignty. Listen as he states his points:

> "...you are sovereign over yourself and a king over your own passions...

> "Masonry is of no Church, but it respects all, so far and so long as they only teach and persuade, and allow

> full freedom of thought and freedom of conscience,
> and the right of private judgement.
>
> "As Masons we deny the right of any church...to
> prescribe to men what they shall believe..."

Masonry, Pike states clearly, is a lawless religion and a "Secret church" that rejects the Holy Bible and relies on the Reason of its members. Their "private judgement," he says, prevails, making them sovereign and unaccountable to the most High God, whom they refuse to name except in secret to the chosen adepts.

Lucifer Said to Be the Source of Light

Incensed and angered over the Christian teaching that man must be subservient to and obey God in all things, Pike goes on to claim that having attained the Light of Freemasonry, man must give recognition to he who bears the light—that is, the "Light–bearer." It is Lucifer who is the source of Light:

> "Lucifer the Light-bearer! Strange and mysterious
> name to give the spirit of Darkness! Lucifer, the Son of
> the Morning! Is it he who bears the Light? Doubt it
> not!"

On page 324, he further describes Lucifer as a Devil: *"...a Devil, the fallen Lucifer, or Light-bearer?"*

This catechism about Lucifer is contained in the pivotal 14th degree for Masonic candidates. In earlier degrees, the Mason is told that the seeking of more and more light is the primary responsibility of Masons. And now he discovers the identity of the Light-bearer. It is Lucifer, or Satan, also known as that old Devil, the Serpent. He is emphatically warned, "Doubt it not!"

The Seething Energies of Lucifer

Manly P. Hall, 33°, the Masonic scholar, gives Masons more information about Lucifer in his important book, *The Lost Keys of Freemasonry*. He writes:

> "When the Mason learns the key to the warrior on the block is the proper application of the dynamo of living power, he has learned the mystery of his Craft.
>
> "The seething energies of Lucifer are in his hands and before he may step onward and upward he must prove his ability to properly apply energy."

The late Anton LaVey, founder in 1966 of the Church of Satan, no doubt agreed with Manly P. Hall, 33°, about the "seething energies of Lucifer" in the hands of Masons. Anton LaVey was a 33rd degree Freemason, as was Aleister Crowley and Michael Aquino, two other infamous Satan worshippers.

Masonry teaches the initiates that its religion is the *"direct descendant of the Ancient Pagan Mysteries"* ("Levi Eliphas," article in *Coil's Masonic Encyclopedia*). And we who are Christians know full well that it is Lucifer who is the Father of these ancient pagan Mysteries.

Again, I ask the Masons who continue to pretend they are Christian as they move up the degree ladder, "Are you dumb, deaf and blind? Do you not see who your Masonic Deity is? Do you think you can freely worship the Great Architect of the Universe as God knowing he is codenamed in Masonry as Abaddon, Jahbulon, and Lucifer? Have you no sense at all?"

Surprisingly, a number of high degree Masons have answered this question. Satan, they admit, is evil, but that is *not* Lucifer. Lucifer is a good angel. Lucifer and Satan, they insist, are two different persons. We Masons honor Lucifer; you Christians think him to be Satan, the Devil. He is not. Lucifer brings us the Light. He is the Light-Bearer. It is, they say, *"he who paved the way for man to advance to godhood."*

These confused Masons point to a recent book, *Pilgrim's Path*, by John Robinson, 33°, in which Robinson attempts to make this same argument. Robinson says that *Isaiah 14*, which mentions "Lucifer," is not about Satan, but has instead been misinterpreted.

What an achievement by Satan, to separate himself from Lucifer in the minds of these deluded men.

Albert Pike, however, was not deluded. He knew the Jewish Kabbalah and he knew who Lucifer was as revealed in the Kabbalah. Lucifer, reveals the Kabbalah, is Satan, the Devil.

ELEVEN

Masons Famous and Infamous

"Each man is his own absolute lawgiver, the dispenser of glory or gloom to himself; the decreer of his life, his reward, his punishment."
—Henry C. Clausen, 33°
"The Idyll of the White Lotus," in
Emergence of the Mystical

I s the above quote by Henry C. Clausen, a modern Sovereign Grand Commander of the Scottish Rite Masonic Lodge, true? Of course not, for it violates the very first of God's Ten Commandments. Some Masons disregard the absurd lies and myths of Freemasonry because they are so enamored of its august and influential membership. They point out to me that "Freemasonry must be a worthy group. Why, just look at the caliber of its membership."

Frankly, Freemasonry has had and continues to have some great personages among it ranks. Many U.S.

Supreme Court Justices were Masons. As many as fourteen U.S. Presidents have been Masons, including George Washington, James Monroe, Andrew Jackson, James Garfield, William McKinley, Teddy Roosevelt, William Howard Taft, Warren Harding, Franklin Roosevelt, Harry Truman, Lyndon Johnson, and Gerald Ford. Some would add Ronald Reagan, William Jefferson Clinton, Barack Obama, and Donald Trump to this list.

There are also the many Vice Presidents, Senators and Congressmen, FBI Directors, cabinet members, and ambassadors. And then there are notables like actors Ernest Borgnine, comedians Red Skelton, Red Buttons and Jack Benny, magician Harry Houdini, baseball player Ty Cobb, writer Mark Twain, astronaut Virgil Grissom, musician and composer Wolfgang Mozart, and patriot, Benjamin Franklin.

But wait...

Hold on, dear friend, true, you will find many famous men who have been and are Freemasons. But you'll also find quite a few very evil and extremely distasteful names on the Masonic rolls as well. Here's just a partial list of unsavory Freemasons:

Karl Marx, founder of Communism

Nathan Bedford Forrest, Confederate General and co-founder of the Ku Klux Klan

John Wilkes Booth, assassin of President Abraham Lincoln

Jesse James, western outlaw

Aleister Crowley, Satanist (called himself "The Beast, 666")

Aleister Crowley, Satanist (called himself "The Beast, 666")

Anders Breivik, mass murderer, Norway.

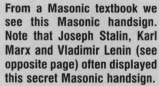

From a Masonic textbook we see this Masonic handsign. Note that Joseph Stalin, Karl Marx and Vladimir Lenin (see opposite page) often displayed this secret Masonic handsign.

SIGN OF THE MASTER OF THE SECOND VEIL.

Benedict Arnold, infamous traitor
Anders Breivik, mass murderer, Norway
Jesse Jackson, Afro-American hustler
Adam Weishaupt, founder of Order of the Illuminati
Joseph Guillotine, inventor of the guillotine
Jimmy Savile, pedophile comedian of Great Britain
Pope Francis, Pontiff, Vatican; apostate
Anton LaVey, founder, Church of Satan
Vladimir Lenin, Communist Leader and mass killer, USSR
Joseph Stalin, Communist Leader and mass killer, USSR

Joseph Stalin, Communist Leader and mass killer, USSR.

Left: Karl Marx, founder of Communism. Right: Vladimir Lenin, Communist Leader and mass killer, USSR. All were Masons.

Great Men Renounce Freemasonry

What Masons want to keep hidden is how many truly great men have over the years renounced and denounced the Masonic Lodge. These men knew that Freemasonry is definitely not a virtuous organization.

President John Quincy Adams: John Quincy Adams, the sixth President of the United States spent over seven years investigating the Masonic Lodge after the "Captain Morgan Affair" in which Captain Morgan, an ex-Mason was stalked and murdered by fellow Masons after revealing the secrets of their handshakes. His throat had been slashed from ear to ear, just as is stated in the Masonic oath all Masons take. Morgan's body was then thrown into a lake. Adams, outraged over this barbaric homicide, writes of his investigation's findings:

> "I saw a Code of Masonic Legislation adapted to prostrate every principle of equal justice, and to corrupt every sentiment of virtuous feeling in the soul of him who bound his allegiance to it. I saw the practice of common honesty, the kindness of Christian benevolence, even the abstinence from atrocious crimes, limited exclusively by lawless oaths, and barbarous penalties, to the social relations between the brotherhood of the Craft. I saw slander organized into a secret, widespread, agency fixing its invisible wings into the heart of the Lodge room. I saw self-invoked invocations of throats cut from ear to ear, of heart and vitals torn out and cast to the wolves and vultures, of skulls smitten off, and hung on spires. I

saw wine drank from a human skull... Such are the
laws of Masonry, such their indelible character, and
with that character perfectly corresponded the history
of the abduction and murder of Morgan, and the
history of Masonic Lodges, chapters, and
encampments, from that day to present." (Adams,
Letters on Freemasonry, reprinted, 2001, Spicewood,
Texas, RiverCrest Publishing)

John Quincy Adams, a dedicated Christian considered
by many to be the most intelligent of all American
Presidents, was a brilliant man, educated in Europe, who
spoke six languages. His father, the famous founding
father John Adams, was the nation's second President.
He also refused to become a Freemason. John Adams
wrote in 1823, after he was President:

"I do conscientiously and since believe that the order
of Freemasonry, if not the greatest, is one of the
greatest moral and political evils under which the
Union is now laboring."

Millard Fillmore, the thirteenth President of the
United States, also considered Freemasonry as a great
evil. He wrote:

"The Masonic fraternity tramples upon our rights,
defeats the administration of justice, and bids
defiance to every government which it cannot
control." (*Presidents of the United States*, Chicago:
National Christian Association, 1953)

John Marshall, America's first Chief Justice of the Supreme Court, left the Lodge after first joining, when he realized its lack of moral bearings. He wrote:

"The institution of Masonry ought to be abandoned as one capable of much evil, and incapable of producing any good..."

True Christian Pastors Speak

Many dedicated Christian Pastors have first joined, then were led by God to renounce Freemasonry. John R. Rice, the well-known Baptist Pastor and author of numerous books is one. In his excellent *Lodges Examined by the Bible*, he tells of many others who also left the Lodge, after being convicted that it was a grievous sin to remain a Mason. Rice found that the Lodges are full of unsaved men, including many who deny the blood of Jesus Christ. He writes:

Repeatedly, from many, many sources I have heard that in Masonic lodges it was not proper for people to pray in the name of Jesus Christ as Saviour and Lord. For instance, I have before me a statement by Mr. Wendell P. Loveless. Mr. Loveless was ex-chaplain of the Masonic Lodge at Wheaton, Illinois. He says:

"I was regularly initiated into seven degrees of the Masonic Order, holding, for a time, the Office of Chaplain in the Blue Lodge, and my knowledge of this society is therefore the result of my experience as a member of it. I now hold a regular demit from the order, which indicates that I was in good and regular standing when I seceded from it." (Page 1, *The Christian and Secret Societies*, by Loveless; National Association)

After showing how he was compelled by the Lord to leave the Masonic Lodge and come out from the unbelievers there, Mr. Loveless says (page 14):

"As Chaplain in the Masonic Lodge, I offered the prayers of the lodge and heard many others offered, but never once in the name of the Lord Jesus Christ. His name is excluded. Certainly it must be very plain that a true believer in Jesus Christ can have no fellowship in that kind of organization. Lodge prayers are not offered in the name of Jesus Christ. The lodge promises the unconverted Jew, the Hindu, the Mohammedan, or any Christ-rejecting sinner who believes there is a Supreme Being, that he may come to the lodge and there find nothing to offend. Since unconverted sinners do not love Jesus Christ, since modernists and rationalists deny that He is the very Son of God, atoning for man's sins, and the only way to salvation, and since Mohammedans and Hindus, like other pagans and heathens, reject Christ and do not accept Him as the Saviour, Son of God and very God, then the lodges shut out Jesus Christ that they may not offend those who hate Him and reject Him!"

A famous Southern Baptist preacher wrote me saying

that in a Masonic Lodge meeting he prayed and was rebuked for offering his petition in the name of Jesus Christ, God's Son, the only Saviour. Because of that rebuke, showing the utterly unchristian and anti-Christian character of the lodges, he discontinued attendance on the lodge.

Martin Wagner, a Pastor who was so convinced of the spiritual dangers of the Lodge that he authored a book, *Freemasonry: An Interpretation*, which exposes the Order, concluded:

"The whole system is a giant evil. We firmly believe it is the greatest foe that the church has to contend against. It insidiously undermines and overthrows the very foundations of evangelical Christianity. Its tendency is to make men indifferent to doctrine and hostile to the positive teaching of Revelation as embodied in the church's creeds and catechisms."

Wagner's contention that the Masonic Lodge "undermines" the Church is justified. Masonry strangles belief in church doctrine and replaces it in the minds and hearts of its members with the fancies and myths of the ancient Mystery religions. It tells the Mason that the Church and the religion of his parents should be abandoned as rank superstition and nonsense. Listen to top Masonic authority W. L. Wilmshurst, 33°, as he insists in his book, *The Masonic Initiation*, that as a man grows, he must cast aside the juvenile superstitious myths of his youth:

"It is well for a man to be born in a Church but terrible for him to die in one; for in religion there must be growth...the elderly man...ought to have outgrown what the Church offers and have attained a higher order of religious life."

Wilmshurst Affirms the Teachings of Rabbi Simeon Bar Yochai, Taught in the 30th Degree

Wilmshurst is, in fact, affirming the warped and unscriptural teachings of the Knight Kadosh, the Man in the Coffin, in the 30th Degree ritual. What horror, what deception is found in these tragic teachings.

That Masonic authority Wilmshurst would affirm the ungodly teachings of kabbalistic Rabbi Simeon Bar Yochai for the 30th Degree is understandable. The Kabbalah and Judaism insist that it is the Jewish RACE that will evolve into godhood. The Jews, and the few Gentiles who follow their pernicious doctrine, will supposedly *perfect* themselves and rise through many incarnations. At perfection, says the Kabbalah, the Jew will become his own Messiah. No need for a Saviour, Jesus.

George Steinmetz, 33° Masonic authority, explains (in the book, *The Truth Twisters*, p. 83, by Harold Berry) that Hindu reincarnation comes from the Jewish Kabbalah, And neither Hindu nor Jewish philosophy, he says "has ever taught of the coming of an individual who would be the 'Saviour,' the Messiah or Redeemer." Instead, these religions and Freemasonry teach that through many incarnations and the slow process of evolution, the initiate will rise to perfection:

"The Messiah, then, will be the final achievement of the plan of the Supreme Architect the—perfection of the race."

Once again we find in the Masonic Lodge the same old lie told to Adam and Eve in the Garden: "Ye shall be as gods."

****

CONCLUSION

Jesus Christ Reveals His Secrets to His Friends of the Christian Church

Of course, Masonry emphasizes that only those Masons who are initiated can learn the hidden secrets of the Masonic Lodge. Only they shall become gods. The Superiors keep secrets from the profane and the undeserving. The Mason must continue to strive toward perfection and work to discover and acquire "more Light." He is trapped. He becomes the unknowing *servant* of evil.

Not so for the Christian. Jesus reveals his secrets to every man who believes in Him. Such men are not treated as servants but as friends.

John 15:15 clearly states: *"Henceforth I call you not servants; for the servant knoweth not what his lord doeth: but I have called you friends; for all things that I have heard of my Father I have made known unto you."*

Oh to be the incomparable friend of Jesus! What a

glory to be encompassed in His Light—the very Light of the world. What a joy to know the unfathomable secrets of our Lord and Saviour, Jesus Christ.

The Church is the Body of Christ. It incorporates the love and wields the power and strength of Jesus Christ. We grow in its compassion and through its concepts and precepts. It is eternal, and so are we, as born again Christians, kept holy and spotless through the might and power of Jesus Christ to whom we give everlasting thanks.

My hope and prayer for Masons is that they will firmly reject the kabbalism of the Masonic Lodge and will truly attain the "Light of the World" by faith in Jesus Christ as Lord and Saviour.

INDEX

ABOUT THE AUTHOR

Well-known author of the #1 national bestseller, *Dark Secrets of The New Age*, Texe Marrs has written books for such major publishers as Simon & Schuster, John Wiley, Prentice Hall/Arco, McGraw-Hill, and Dow Jones-Irwin. His books have sold millions of copies. He is one of the world's foremost symbologists and is a first-rate scholar of ancient history and Mystery religions.

Texe Marrs was assistant professor of aerospace studies, teaching American defense policy, strategic weapons systems, and related subjects at the University of Texas at Austin for five years. He has also taught international affairs, political science, and psychology for two other universities. A graduate *summa cum laude* from Park College, Kansas City, Missouri, he earned his Master's degree at North Carolina State University.

As a career USAF officer (now retired), he commanded communications-electronics and engineering units. He holds a number of military decorations including the Vietnam Service Medal and Presidential Unit Citation, and has served in Germany, Italy, and throughout Asia.

Texe Marrs is heard globally on his popular, international internet radio program, *Bible Home Church (www. biblehomechurch.org)*.

FOR OUR NEWSLETTER

Power of Prophecy offers a free sample newsletter focusing on world events, false religion, and secret societies, cults, and the occult challenge to Christianity. If you would like to receive this newsletter, please write to:

Power of Prophecy
4819 R.O. Drive, Suite 102
Spicewood, Texas 78669

You may also e-mail your request to:
customerservice1@powerofprophecy.com

FOR OUR WEBSITE

The *Power of Prophecy* newsletter is published free monthly on our website. This website has descriptions of all Texe Marrs' books, and are packed with interesting, insight-filled articles, videos, breaking news, and other information. You also have the opportunity to order an exciting array of books, tapes, and videos through our online Catalog and Sales Store. Visit our website at:

www.powerofprophecy.com

SHORTWAVE RADIO PROGRAM

Power of Prophecy's international radio program is broadcast weekly on shortwave radio throughout the United States and the world. *Power of Prophecy* can be heard on WWCR at 4.840 on Sunday nights at 9:00 p.m. Central Time. You may also listen to *Power of Prophecy* 24/7 on website *powerofprophecy.com*.

OTHER BOOKS BY RIVERCREST PUBLISHING

For additional books by Texe Marrs, please see *page vi*

Behind Communism, *by Frank L. Britton*

Bohemian Grove: Cult of Conspiracy, *by Mike Hanson*

Gods of the Lodge, *by Reginald C. Haupt, Jr.*

Letters on Freemasonry, *by John Quincy Adams*

Matrix of Gog: From the Land of Magog Came the Khazars to Destroy and Plunder, *by Daniel Patrick*

New Age Lies to Women, *by Wanda Marrs*

On the Jews and Their Lies, *by Martin Luther*

Protocols of the Learned Elders of Zion

Synagogue of Satan, *by Andrew Carrington Hitchcock*

For additional information we highly recommend
the following website:

www.powerofprophecy.com

MORE RESOURCES FOR YOU

Books:

(For all orders, please include shipping and handling charge)

Conspiracy of the Six-Pointed Star—Eye Opening Revelations and Forbidden Knowledge About Israel, the Jews, Zionism, and the Rothschilds, by Texe Marrs (432 pages) $25

Codex Magica—Secret Signs, Mysterious Symbols, and Hidden Codes of the Illuminati, by Texe Marrs (624 pages, large format) $35

DNA Science and the Jewish Bloodline, by Texe Marrs (256 pages) $20

Gods of the Lodge, by Reginald C. Haupt, Jr (195 pages) $15

Hidden Secrets of the Eastern Star, by Dr. Cathy Burns (491 pages) $20

Holy Serpent of the Jews, by Texe Marrs (224 pages) $20

Letters on Freemasonry, by John Quincy Adams (334 page) $20

Masonic and Occult Symbols Illustrated, by Dr. Cathy Burns (543 pages) $20

Mysterious Monuments—Encyclopedia of Secret Illuminati Designs, Masonic Architecture, and Occult Places, by Texe Marrs (624 pages, large format) $35

Protocols of the Learned Elders of Zion (320 Pages) $20

The Synagogue of Satan, by Andrew Carrington Hitchcock (320 pages) $20

<u>Videos:</u>

Cauldron of Abaddon—"From Jerusalem and Israel Flow a Torrent of Satanic Evil and Mischief Endangering the Whole World" by Texe Marrs (DVD) $25

The Eagle Has Landed!—Magic, Alchemy, and the Illuminati Conquest of Outer Space by Texe Marrs (DVD) $25

Illuminati Mystery Babylon—The Hidden Elite of Israel, America, and Russia, and Their Quest for Global Dominion by Texe Marrs (DVD) $25

Masonic Lodge Over Jerusalem—The Hidden Rulers of Israel, the Coming World War in the Middle East and the Rebuilding of the Temple by Texe Marrs (DVD) $25

Secret Societies and the Illuminati by Texe Marrs (DVD) $20

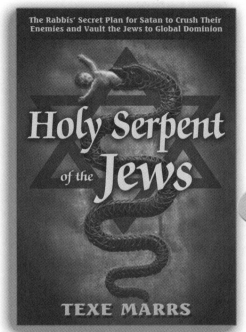

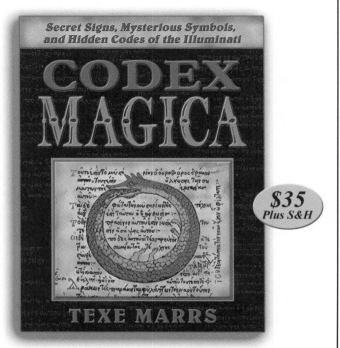